Whiskers, WAGS, AND WOOFS

A Life, Repurposed Compilation

Whiskers,

POEMS AND HEARTFELT ESSAYS

WAGS, AND

FOR DOG AND CAT LOVERS

WOOFS

MICHELLE RAYBURN
AND FRIENDS

FAITH CREATIVITY
LIFE BOOKS

Whiskers, Wags, and Woofs
Copyright ©2024 Michelle Rayburn
ISBN: 978-1-954576-08-7
Published by Faith Creativity Life Books (FCL Books)
www.fclbooks.com

Some names have been changed to protect identities.

Compiled and edited by Michelle Rayburn – michellerayburn.com
Cover, typesetting, and e-book by Michelle Rayburn – missionandmedia.com

For Copper

Contents

Comfort and Support

Playful Antics and Adventure

Foreword

KATHY CARLTON WILLIS

'VE HEARD IT SAID THAT if you believed in reincarnation, you'd want to come back as the pet of a childless couple. I can't have human children, so I grin at that statement. Obviously, our pets aren't reincarnated, but I can say our fur kids have had the best life. We've had two cats and five dogs (and also a guinea pig, which has whiskers, so it counts, right?). Let's explore some of the blessings of our four-legged friends.

Emotional Support

Even though we indulge our fur family, it is never more than what they give to us. I don't have an official emotional support animal, but all my pets have provided wonderful support. We give them security blankets, and they give us the emotional version of a blankie. (Our Jazzy used to even suck on the edge of her baby blanket!)

I've needed even more emotional support after having to say goodbye to each of our dear pets. Some of the authors in this book have experienced this same sort of separation grief. It's such a permanent sense of loss. Each routine at home reminds you of the last goodbye. No exuberant greeting at the door. No loving presence nestled in by you on the couch. (Yes, we allow that!) No game and treat time. Just silence. But the stories of their lives make it worth risking the sadness of those goodbyes.

Escape Artists

There are other emotions when it comes to our fur kin. When one of our pets escapes and runs away, it can cause quite a panic! I've been on more than one search party for our dogs. Mandy was lost for two weeks (supposedly let loose by my disgruntled boss's wife). We got her back! Our mostly black Boston Terrier Mijo got out several times, learning to be a quite skilled escape artist. Finding him was especially challenging after dark. Pro tip: we found that driving our car slowly, opening the door upon spotting him, and then yelling, "Car ride!" helped. That always enticed him to quit running and jump in for his next adventure. He didn't realize his next adventure was home!

In this book, you'll read about other search parties and feel the author's emotion as if your own dog were loose. It isn't surprising that our pets bond to us with deep soul connections.

In Sync

These incredible creatures are so in tune with us. I'll never forget the night Jazzy had her one and only seizure. That same night, I had a dangerous drop in my blood glucose. I can't help but wonder if her seizure happened because she sensed it.

In the book, we hear stories from several authors about how their pets can sense their suffering or worries. They not only sink into our hearts, but they are also in sync with our hearts.

Communication Expert

Speaking of connecting with our hearts, my Hettie (our current Boston Terrier) knows how to work it. She does this cute "tap tap" with her paw on our legs to get our attention and ask for whatever she has on her mind. And she speaks just fine without using English. I guess she uses Hettie-ish! But she sure *understands* English, even when she's busy doing something else while we're talking, and she overhears us. We are blown away by how many words she knows! (Even the vet was impressed. Yes, now I've resorted to bragging! What pet parent doesn't?) Our lives sure are enriched by our doggies, aren't they?

Entertainment

In addition to the tender and touching moments, our pets also provide comic relief. Hettie has a boyfriend. Or maybe she thinks he is a son. It's hard to say. Our condo shares a wall with our neighbor. Nancy walks Georgie a couple of times a day and goes right by our windows.

Perched atop the back of the sofa, looking out our front window, Hettie watches for Georgie. Georgie is a five-pound miniature Maltese puppy. Hettie knows when it's time for Georgie's walk. When she sees him, she lets out her own special cry, just for Georgie. Then she races through the house and bursts out the doggie door in a hurry to get to sniff him through the fence.

When Georgie is in his backyard, Hettie goes outdoors to rest on her side of the barrier to be near him. Or they sniff noses under the fence. They have a conversation and are content to rest on each side of the wall, knowing their bestie is just on the other side of the cedar. Hettie has knocked down grass in the very impression of her resting body, evidence that she is happy to have Georgie time in any way she can. Even though Hettie weighs twenty pounds more and has five years on Georgie, they are best friends. She's mostly black; he's all white. The contrasts between them are hilarious.

I can't really explain it, but there's just something about their relationship that makes me grin. Georgie's mommy is amused by the special friendship too, and we've already had a couple of play dates. When we say his name, Hettie's ears perk up and her radar ears turn, hoping to hear his sweet baby bark. Her whole body engages in the hunt for Georgie. A mohawk of fur erupts from her spine as she prances and sings a little whimpery song of longing. Anticipation is a big deal in Hettie's world.

Not only does Hettie love play dates, but she also likes making up games.

Pizza Bones

Food games are a source of entertainment in our household. When we eat pizza, I don't eat the edge of the crust, and I give Hettie what we call the "pizza bones." Recently, I gave her two. I handed one crust to her and put one where she could get it later. With pizza bone clenched in her teeth, she ran through the house, looking for a hiding spot to pretend bury it! We heard the clip-clip of her nails as she shopped for the perfect place. But then she ran back to the second pizza bone, and, while keeping the one already in her mouth, she scooped up the other and had *both* in her jaws at the same time. These are the poofy rise-up pizzas, so they weren't wimpy pizza bones.

Hettie was so proud of herself. Honestly, we were proud of her too! She has a tiny smoosh-face muzzle, so it was quite an accomplishment. She *really* pranced around after that, and then, as if a lightbulb went off above her head, she went clip-clip-clip out the doggie door to bury the pizza bones for real. No pretending this time!

Love Overflowing

These creatures with whiskers, wags, and woofs sure deliver a bigger-than-life package of love and joy. Their silly antics are such day brighteners, and their loving support comforts us even on our worst days. When they show off their tricks, it seems like *something* is going right in our world.

As you read through the book, you'll grin at the stories shared. Your heart will feel the nuzzle of God's presence, available for your comfort and peace. I encourage you to stop and commemorate the heartwarming times your pets have provided special moments. Thank God for his blessings—the whiskers, wags, and woofs as well as the other gifts he's brought your way.

Hettie

Known as God's Grin Gal, **KATHY CARLTON WILLIS** writes and speaks with a balance of funny and faith, whimsy and wisdom. Kathy is passionate about helping believers have aha! moments with the application of Scripture. Her words inspire grin-worthy moments despite groan-worthy experiences. Explore Kathy's Grin Gal line of books, where you'll spot her Boston Terrier logo—pet approved. Her boldly practical tips, tools, and takeaways sound like her friendship chats while walking Hettie. www.kathycarltonwillis.com

Unforgettable Friendships

Love Unleashed in a Golden

MICHELLE RAYBURN

WHAT DOES IT TAKE TO be a dog whisperer? It isn't so much that any certain person has special powers over canines or any other four-pawed creatures, for that matter. Anyone can learn to speak a dog's language because there really are no words. Yes, there are commands and calls and reprimands. However, I'm talking about the dialect that transcends letters and words, where human and pooch comprehend perfectly. There are no complicated phrases or verbs to conjugate. Nothing to spell or memorize. There is only one message: love.

Dogs—and cats too—just know when we love them. And we know when they love us. Love emanates from the warmth in our eyes and the smiles on our faces, through gentle hands stroking velvety ears, and in the welcoming essence flowing from our hearts. They just *feel* the love, soak in it, and then send it right back through twinkly, coffee-colored eyes, through wagging tails, snuggles and purrs, and exuberant kisses. They'll run right up to the dog lover in the room before anyone makes a move. Dogs *know*. This symbiotic exchange is what it means to be a whisperer. And I've always fancied myself to be one.

So, it would make perfect sense that I would be a lifelong dog owner, the model "pawrent" to fur kids with speckles and freckles, whiskers, slobber, and paws.

However, I am not.

My only adventure with one Cocker Spaniel didn't go how I wanted it to. Sadie Alexandria—dubbed Satan by my husband—was a purebred that came into our family as a puppy when I was a full-time nurse working long hours. Choosing a living bundle of energy as a means of resisting baby fever at the summit of graduating from college and launching a career is not a recommended path. Human-canine bliss did not ensue.

Sadie spent too much time in a kennel, an afterthought when I got too busy. The vet scolded me on more than one occasion for the pup's office-visit behavior as a nervous and skittish nipper, and we got sent to doggie obedience school. Her anxiety in the horse arena with all the other dogs in training became a nervous poop-fest, with me stopping to collect her deposits frequently as we walked the loop and followed commands. Well, *I* followed the trainer's commands. However, my canine companion constantly crouched, gawked over her shoulder, eying the other dogs—who were all listening marvelously to their owners—and tucked her tail between her legs.

We had challenges at home too. Sadie preferred to poop inside the house instead of outside in the lovely yard we trimmed and mowed. I couldn't even walk across the street to get the mail without her separation anxiety prompting an accident—I mean, an "on-purpose."

AFTER A COUPLE OF YEARS, a pink line on a stick changed Sadie's life forever. We were expecting our first baby. She still piddled whenever company came over and yipped and nipped when anyone other than me tried to pet her. Maternity leave was rough.

Sadie didn't adjust well to having a new baby in the family, and I didn't trust her around him. I finally knew she would need to be rehomed. I sobbed—postpartum hormones are not a good time for rehoming your beloved "fur-child." But we found a young couple with no children who had just lost their Cocker Spaniel. And she, too, had been a bundle of nerves. Saying goodbye nearly broke me, but it was best for Sadie.

After that experience, I never adopted another dog of my own. Instead, I've cuddled and coddled from afar, been Auntie to my sister's beloved fur daughters, and become the dog-sitter eager to help friends and family. I keep dog bowls in my kitchen to be ready for creature company. Nothing dims a dog whisperer's love for wagging tails, lapping tongues, and silly antics.

> Nothing dims a dog whisperer's love for wagging tails, lapping tongues, and silly antics.

ENTER COPPER. THIS GOLDEN RETRIEVER is the epitome of joy wrapped in fur. He's like a living sunbeam, radiating amber rays of happiness, with an infectious zest for life. His wagging tail is a perpetual metronome of excitement, always thumping back and forth, tapping out a greeting as he stands, tennis ball in mouth, waiting for the party to begin.

I also happen to be Copper's grandpawrent—pronounced "grand-paw-rent." He lives just a mile up the road, and I'm surprised he hasn't figured out how to get to my house through the woods and over the hill. His mom says he barks—something he rarely does—and races to wait by the door whenever she says, "Do you want to go to Grandma's?"

When Copper's humans go out of town, he hangs out with Grandpa and Grandma. Grandpa has never called him Satan. In fact, he sneaks Copper little treats and throws the ball outside. As grandpawrents, we have also discovered a beautiful benefit to being the dog *sitters* rather than the dog *owners*. We don't pay the bills. No groomer visits. No vet bills. No bags of food or obedience classes to budget for.

We get to enjoy all the cuddles rent-free. When Copper rests his head on my lap or nudges my hand to rub his ears, I get all the endorphins without the obligations. He's eager to please and ridiculously smart. And I'm not just saying that because he's family.

> We get to enjoy all the cuddles rent-free.

Copper knows I head to my home office every morning after I grab my coffee. So now, while I'm in the shower, he heads to the office ahead of me and chooses his spot on the soft white rug. He's right there waiting as soon as I blow-dry my hair and grab the coffee. I don't need a smartwatch to tell me it's time to stand up and stretch. Copper nudges my elbow and begs for a nose massage if I sit too long. And if I start a Zoom meeting, he's sure to pop on camera to see who's there.

Someone also has Grandma twisted around his little paw. He will leave his dog food untouched in the bowl until I start to worry about whether he feels OK or not. And then, when I head to the refrigerator for a beverage or a snack, there he is. He sits, sometimes even tries all the tricks with high-fives and shakes and spins. Then it hits me. *He wants cheese.* Sure enough. A few sprinkles of shredded cheddar on top of his kibble, and he scarfs it all down, licks the bowl, and washes it down with a splash of water. I haven't yet taught him how to say "Excuse me" for the belch that follows.

It's nice to be so loved unconditionally. Except for my human grandchildren, no one else is as excited to see me as Copper is when he comes running to heap on the love. That Retriever is always up for a welcoming party.

When I stop over to visit Copper and his humans at his house, he knocks over the grandchildren playing outside as he charges to greet me the moment I get out of my car, sometimes standing up to attempt to give a kiss on the cheek or place his paws possessively on my shoulders. Then, he gets the zoomies and races around the yard in crazy delight for a few minutes before returning for a belly rub.

These stops have taught me that grandpawrents should never wear white pants—they get muddy paw prints from affectionate greetings. Black pants are out too. They show the fur—also from affectionate greetings.

I WANTED TO PUBLISH THIS book because pet lovers of all kinds can delight in the simple pleasures of loving fluffy beasts with whiskers and tails—whether they live in our homes or we appreciate their presence in the corners of our world. Maybe you pet every canine at the park, share regular playful moments with your neighbor's pup, or volunteer at an animal shelter. Perhaps you work in a place that has therapy dog visits, or you leave a bowl of food out for the kitty that keeps looking in your windows. Side note: one cat took a year off my life on a summer night when its massive furry face popped up in my open office window. I'm pretty sure it tried to say, "I hear you're the snack lady." I wasn't "a-mewsed."

> They bring laughter, love, and a whole
> lot of golden magic into our days.

It does a human good to have friends like Copper, who bring laughter, love, and a whole lot of golden magic into our days. And it never hurts to tell their stories, even the failures and the lessons they taught us about ourselves. They show us the meaning of words such as lighthearted, lively, boisterous, raucous, rollicking, euphoric, and saucy. They also have a lot to teach humans about how to love others. And for their profound impact, we thank pets with a few bites of our lunch, a quick scritch behind the ears, or a simple snuggle on the sofa. That's a pretty good deal, if you ask me.

MICHELLE RAYBURN, the publisher and managing editor of this book, is married to her high school sweetheart, Phil, is mom to two thirty-something sons, and adores their wives. She has four grandchildren—and counting. Michelle hosts the *Midlife Repurposed* podcast and writes humor, Christian living books, and Bible studies. Dark chocolate, an iced coffee, and a good book in the hammock top her favorites list—especially if there's a visiting pup to watch bunnies and squirrels and share the backyard.

Almost Normal

SANDY LIPSKY

MAPLE'S MOM WAS FOUND NEAR a dumpster when an alert Good Samaritan rescued her before she delivered. The adoption process for our "garbage dog" was comparable to when we adopted our daughter. References were necessary, along with photographs of our home and backyard, and a detailed description of where she would sleep. The only question not asked was how we intended to educate her. Texts went back and forth between the Humane Society and us for weeks. After answering the question of why we wanted this puppy, my husband and I received the joyful news. We could come pick her up. Fingerprints not required.

> *Best in Show* is not in her future, but unconditional love is.

The reason to add Maple to our family wasn't because of pedigree or beauty. Circular and centered like a crown, a huge cowlick adorns the top of her tiny head. The projection of her upper front teeth causes our veterinarian to say, "That's quite an overbite," each time we go for an appointment. Her legs are stubby, and her body is long. *Best in Show* is not in her future, but unconditional love is.

What Were We Thinking?

While in Mexico on vacation, I scrolled through a pet adoption website. We had always been a one-dog family but agreed our playful pup needed a buddy. As I searched, my finger stopped mid-swipe. The dark, beseeching eyes met mine. I gasped. She was the most beautiful dog I had ever seen. There was no way she was still available. On a whim, and with my husband's approval, I contacted the listed number. Within an hour, I received a reply.

> She was the most beautiful dog I had ever seen.

After only a few back-and-forth texts, we arranged plans to meet the dog. Listed as an eight-month-old shepherd mix, she looked gentle and friendly—a perfect sibling for Maple. Not wanting anyone else to swoop in before us, we scheduled the visit for the day after we returned from our vacation.

The scheduled get-together would take place at a location an hour and a half drive from our home. To prepare for our trip, we dosed Maple with medicine to settle her stomach. Next, we stopped at a local pet store to pick up necessities. With a new crate, leash, and toy, we felt ready for the outing.

Our GPS guided us to a well-manicured ranch-style home with a fenced backyard. I turned to my husband, smiled, and took a deep breath. "Here we go." As I stepped out of the car, I heard a man's voice call out from the direction of an open window.

"She's waiting for you in the backyard."

"OK. Thank you."

Not sure what to do with Maple, Jon encouraged me to walk down the driveway to the wrought iron gate to the backyard. He would wait by the fence until I gave him the green light.

A middle-aged, dark-haired woman with a kind smile walked toward me. She invited me to have a seat. My head turned side to side as I checked out the landscape and looked for our dog. With a casual wave, I let Jon know he and Maple could come. A white, medium-sized dog greeted them at the gate. His tail wagged as he performed the canine sniff reception, and then he ran to join another dog. "That's Janie," the kind woman said as her sleeveless arm pointed to the back of her wooded yard.

With a whistle and a treat in hand, the rescue mom was able to coax Janie toward us. The full-grown puppy with white fur and brown patches gave us a wide berth and approached the woman with a tucked tail and lowered head. She gave the impression of a soldier getting low to the ground to avoid discovery in enemy territory. The offered snack disappeared with a lick. Then she backed away and fled to the friendly white dog, who we now knew to be her brother.

This repeated series of events went on for the next thirty minutes. When she seemed more at ease, I held out a treat. Her pink tongue could not dislodge the morsel from my lowered, open hand because of the distance between us. When Jon held out multiple treats, she acted as if a lightning bolt would strike her if she got too close to him.

"She's afraid of men, but she is warming up to my husband," the foster mom said.

Maple let out a low and steady growl each time Janie came near her. Instructed not to look her in the eye, we continued chatting as if this was not a monumental decision we needed to make in the next hour. The new toy we offered caused her to cower as a child would if presented with a stalk of broccoli. In a stuttering voice, I inquired if the plain white dog was available for adoption.

"No. He's already spoken for."

The time for our decision came. The rescue worker leaned forward in her chair and looked me in the eye.

"What do you think? Is there anything preventing you from taking her home today?"

Jon turned his face toward mine and tilted his head. After thirty-six years of marriage, I felt confident I knew what his eyes were communicating. I nodded.

"We'll take her."

> Our decision still surprises me. It made zero sense.

Our decision still surprises me. It made zero sense. Maple didn't like her. Janie was afraid of us. It was a hunch. We saw what she could be.

Once we signed the documents and made the payment, the foster mom, the only human who could touch her, lifted her into our car. The regeneration of Janie had begun.

Rough Start

Getting her out of the crate took coaxing when we arrived home. Another forty-five minutes to go from the garage to the backyard. Once home, Maple warmed up to her new sister. They ran around our fenced backyard before Janie stopped and rolled in the poop I hadn't thought to pick up. As I screeched, she bolted for our pool and fell in. Jon dashed over to guide her to the stairs. She scrambled onto the pool deck, shook, and dashed to the back barrier. In a Herculean move, she attempted to leap over the six-foot wooden enclosure. Not a Hallmark movie moment.

Neither of us could touch her, so we trusted the sun to dry her off. How would we ever be able to get her back into the house?

Treats. The foster mom suggested savory bacon-type lures. While Jon kept an eye on both dogs, I headed to the store for snacks. Lots of snacks. This was going to be a long day.

It took two hours of laying pepperoni tasty treats down like Dr. Doolittle to get her in the house. The ingenuity of three adults—our daughter and us—finally trumped the fear of an eight-month-old stray. Janie stayed so busy avoiding us that by bedtime, a few treats inside her crate won her over. My husband and I flopped into bed, closed our eyes, and knew no more until loud heaving noises woke us up. All the cajoling food lay in a heaping pile on the floor of the crate.

Our veterinarian gave us little hope Janie would ever be normal. "She is well past the age of when puppies are socialized."

My body froze. I couldn't look the doctor in the eye. *No hope?*

The vet made a few suggestions after noticing my wide-eyed stare. She recommended a dog trainer. Time at doggy daycare at the clinic was set up for once a week. The doctor hoped that with an abundance of exposure to people and fun treats, Janie would learn to enjoy human contact.

> With unconditional love, devoted training, and doggy daycare, she has truly joined the family.

Transformation

One year later, Janie is almost normal. She still has days where she pulls back from an outreached hand. I don't know if she will ever let me put on her harness without a chase around the kitchen table either. But with unconditional love, devoted training, and doggy daycare, she has truly joined the family. Our daughter was the first to pet her after a month in our home. It took one year for her to not recoil at my husband's outreached hand. In twelve months, Janie learned how to chew a bone, play fetch, and snuggle on the couch. When a child pedals a bike past her, she no longer runs away like a crazed, spooked stallion—leaping over an eight-foot fence.

LIKE MAPLE AND JANIE, I'M flawed. Maple on the outside, Janie on the inside, and me—I'm messed up on the inside and out. The Bible tells me God loves me. Unconditionally. No matter the depth of my imperfections. Knowing this truth is regenerative. It gives me hope and freedom to live up to my potential. Just as I have seen in our pups, I, too, can thrive under unconditional love.

SANDY LIPSKY tries to sit still and compose the things God whispers in her ear. By day, she writes, teaches piano, and cares for her household. Nighttime finds her reading. Her latest work appears in a compilation entitled Renewed Christmas Blessings. Sandy is also a contributing author for several WordGirls devotional books and essay compilations. She enjoys Georgia's seasons and spending time with her husband, daughter, and puppies Maple and Janie. www.sandylipsky.com

She Picked Me

SHEILA PRESTON FITZGERALD

I DIDN'T KNOW IT AT THE time, but God orchestrated every detail of our union when we first laid eyes on one another in mid-June 2004. In my search for a small, non-shedding dog, I was led to a kind, older couple who had an excellent reputation as small dog breeders. The Bichon-Frise, described as a happy lap dog, was their specialty. They bred a petite version of this lovable little dog.

The breeder and I arranged a day and time for me to meet the new litter and their parents. I was highly impressed with the breeders, their facility, their program, and their care for the animals. When I walked into the meeting room for the first time, a pile of six-week-old puppies frolicked and tumbled at my feet. I was in heaven.

I don't remember how many there were—more than six but no more than ten. Tiny, one-pound balls of white fur pounced, jumped, rolled, and played about me. They were so little and so busy that I was afraid I'd step on one. I found a spot on the floor and sat down. Within seconds, they were all over me. My face is smiling, and my heart is expanding as I recall the precious memory now.

The hardest part was figuring out which one to choose. The pups all looked exactly alike—solid white balls of fur with adorable fat pink bellies, piercing black eyes, a black nose, and black lips that smiled back at me. And the smell! What is it about the alluring smell of puppies? It makes me giddy, and I regress into a childlike state of joy whenever I'm around them.

> What is it about the alluring smell of puppies?

I picked up every single one of them and ran them through my version of puppy tests. I tugged on ears. I put my fingers inside their ears. I pulled on tails. I held them up to see if they'd make eye contact. I rolled them over onto their backs. I held them on my chest. I held them on my lap. I looked in their mouths and rubbed around their tiny mouths, noses, and eyes. Of course, most of them thought I was playing, and that was A-OK. I was looking for any sign of injury, illness, and temperament issues. All the puppies did really well, making it even more difficult to pick just one.

After some time, I thought I'd settled on which little ball of white fur would be mine, and I decided to let them all play again with their litter mates. Still sitting on the floor, I waited to see if any puppies would be willing to leave their mates and come to me. It didn't take long, less than a minute, before one—only one—came to me as I sat still and waited.

I wanted a female. She was a girl pup. She crawled up onto my legs, up to my chest, and straight into my heart. She passed every single puppy test. When I rolled the tiny one-pound-three-ounce puppy onto her back, she stared into my eyes as if to say, "I'm yours! I pick YOU to give my love, my service, and my life to." Unlike her litter mates, she didn't quickly get distracted and leave me to go play with the others. She stayed content, cradled in my arms.

THE BREEDERS HAD A POLICY with their puppies; potential owners could view and pick out a pup at six weeks of age when their little personalities developed, but the new owner was not allowed to take theirs home until it was nine weeks old. The breeder found this policy to be the best for the pups' social development for the long term. It made sense.

Because every puppy looked exactly alike, it would have been extremely difficult to know, outside of male versus female, which puppy I had chosen. As a professional manicurist, I had a supply of nail polish, which contained an OPI Collection line of "pawlish"—a one-coat, quick-dry nail polish primarily used on kids' nails. The "pawlish" collection was a marketing spin-off from the movie *Legally Blonde 2*, in which Reese Witherspoon's character protects her beloved pup's mother from animal testing. Knowing the breeder's policy ahead of time, I had grabbed a bottle of "pawlish" and threw it in my handbag before I left home—just in case.

After the tiny ball of fur—that literally fit in the palm of my hand—picked me and I paid the deposit fee, I asked the breeder if I could polish a couple of her toenails. "Of course. She's yours now," they replied. I rolled my pup onto her back in the palm of my left hand. She lay still and trusted me to mess with her itty-bitty toenails. She even let me blow on her nails. The polish was designed to dry almost instantly, and it did just that. We snuggled a bit longer. I didn't want to leave her. I knew we were meant to be each other's. Little did I know, at that time, how true that would become.

THE NEXT THREE WEEKS SEEMED to drag by. I couldn't wait to bring my little love home. Doubts crept in. *Did the polish stay on? Would she remember me? What if there was a mix-up, and somehow, she went to someone else?*

Finally, the day arrived to make the return drive to the neighboring state. I was full of nervous excitement. Again, the same doubts and questions rolled through my mind. I could not wait to sit on the floor among the puppies and see if "my" pup would pick me a second time.

OH, Y'ALL. GOD COULD NOT have orchestrated it any better than he did. As I sat on the floor, the litter of pups came to investigate but quickly went back to playing with one another.

All but one.

The Lord chose her specifically for me. He knew there would come a day when I would be lost and wandering in the darkness of trauma, suffering, and pain. Is it not amazing how God knows our needs and prepares the way, even before we know we need it?

> God really did choose her for me.

Slowly, with a bit of reservation, I rolled the soft ball of white fur over onto its back. Tears filled my eyes when I saw it—two polished toenails. God really did choose her for me. He knew how desperately I'd need her in years to come when I would become a high-trauma amputee with compound, bilateral permanent damage to both of my legs. God knew she would become the sweetest, most loyal registered support animal, who would go with me everywhere, and the dearest companion and loving family member. He made sure she picked me not once but twice!

God used that little ball of white fluff to teach me numerous life lessons over the next eighteen years. Never having had children of my own, she was and is one of the greatest gifts I've ever received. I thank God for the priceless gift of Daisy's unconditional love.

I miss her deeply.

By the way, do you know what color of polish I used on Daisy's toenails that first day? Sapphire blue. A color I would have never used on a girl dog. For those who don't know my story or my book, *One Foot in Heaven*, sapphire blue represents the gift of life and the Holy Spirit, who presented to me the night of my near-death, life-altering motorcycle accident.

God knew.

In loving memory of: Daisy Mae Fitzgerald "Sweet pea"
5/5/2004–7/25/2022

SHEILA PRESTON FITZGERALD, author, speaker, and tragedy coach, is alive today only by the grace of God. A near-death motorcycle accident that should have taken her life, instead, filled this godly woman with a passion larger than life itself. Sheila's love of people, love of life, and most importantly her love for Jesus, radiates in all she does. www.OneFootInHeavenOnline.com

The King

ANDREW LEIPOLD

P HARAOH GREETED ME WITH A skepticism reserved for new boyfriends or stepparents in clichéd movies. He had been the man in my wife Leah's life for five years before I arrived, and like any good dog, Pharaoh knew he was in charge.

During that time, Pharaoh lived a carefree existence. He sneered at the idea of training and preferred to teach you how things went. My arrival coincided with our time in law school and its associated stressors. In response, Pharaoh donned a second hat. He was no longer just a companion for Leah; instead, he was a partner in the ways we all hope to be for those we love.

Pharaoh became more affectionate. He owned the anxiety and wore it with a steadily growing beard of gray fur. He remained a constant regardless of early mornings and late nights. And like any good partner, Pharaoh would tell you when he felt things had gone too far. After a particularly tough stretch of school, he let Leah know he felt neglected. Pharaoh, ever the nuanced communicator, took her bedroom slippers, ripped them into pieces, and gently laid them on her pillows for her to see when she got home.

As a young dog, Pharaoh was in peak physical condition. He earned his name after bossing around the other members of his litter. His muscles rippled through his coarse brown fur as he bounded through the backyard in response to any squirrel or deer who dared enter. He was stout—barrel-chested with a shock of white fur on his chest—and fluctuated between sixty and sixty-five pounds. Some mixture of Rhodesian Ridgeback caused the fur on his back to rise and darken at a perceived threat, but we never established his breed despite DNA tests for dogs gaining popularity. Pharaoh and I shared a silent understanding that he scoffed at such things. Competing strands of DNA were irrelevant to Pharoah; he was simply, yet perfectly, a dog.

> Competing strands of DNA were irrelevant to Pharoah; he was simply, yet perfectly, a dog.

I grew up around dogs and knew I could soften Pharaoh's stance toward me. I began doing the simple things: I walked him, ran with him, threw him tennis balls, played tug of war, and snuck in a few treats. We developed a bond that led to me occasionally being given his head rather than his butt when he joined us on the couch at night.

Walks with Pharaoh carried equal parts danger and humor. When Pharaoh was on a leash, any dog in sight was a personal affront. He lunged at other dogs to ensure your grip strength was true, and nothing angered him more than a dog of similar stature. His sense of humor came into play whenever a dog barked at him while stuck inside. Hearing their call, Pharaoh would pause, look in their direction, and pee directly into their yard with just the right combination of sass and innocence.

After we graduated, I joined the military, and Pharaoh continued his trek around the country. Hailing from South Carolina originally, he spent years in Georgia and Texas before we settled back in Georgia. When I returned from a deployment, Pharaoh made one thing quite clear: never again. By that point, it had become, "Never again, *Dad.*" I passed the unknowable tests and returned the favors he did for Leah by becoming a constant in his life. Even as he neared ten years of age, Pharaoh showed no signs of slowing down. He fought armadillos, got sprayed after skunks tunneled under our home, and delivered a possum to our door.

Pharaoh was smart about the fights he picked. When it came to deer, Pharaoh pretended he wanted to engage with an animal twice his size, which he knew he could not get to because of a fence. Like any good dog, he reserved a special hatred for cats. I initially thought the fireman rescue of a cat in a tree was an overplayed sitcom joke. Now, I can tell you it takes on a different feeling when you and your wife are hiding in your house and peering through the blinds to observe the rescue caused by your dog.

During our time in the military, we were expecting our first child. Dogs know when something is up, and Pharaoh laid on, around, and generally as close to Leah's stomach as possible. We had zero concerns about Pharaoh adapting when our son, Hank, was born. For all his feeling-out processes and initial hesitations with adults, he had an unconditional love for kids. Hank grew and grew, and they began developing the timeless bond between a boy and his dog.

> They began developing the timeless bond between a boy and his dog.

Throughout Pharaoh's life, he stayed young. Neighbors repeated his age with a question mark as he pranced throughout the neighborhood. This continued until his twelfth year with us, when we began to experience some of the difficulties of caring for an aging dog. He began having kidney issues, and his willingness to exercise and play became a daily question. The nights resembled those with a newborn as Pharaoh's nails clicked across our old hardwood floors at all hours. We got up frequently to let him out and tried to ease the coughing and vomiting that had become a regular occurrence.

> Despite his pain, his stubbornness never relented.

Despite his pain, his stubbornness never relented. His vet prescribed a new diet, and Pharaoh behaved like any good patient. He let me buy the food, feigned compliance, and promptly began a hunger strike. I quickly relented, and Pharaoh knew he had the upper hand. Never one to let a moment pass, Pharaoh pretended to hate his original food until it was properly seasoned with wet food, and we embarked together on a clandestine agreement to politely ignore the vet's advice.

Things took a turn for the worse when Pharaoh's seizures began. The lack of control struck fear in our hearts. His condition required us to monitor him like a hawk and deal with the reality that we could face a tough decision at any moment. We prayed for wisdom and a sign. For about a month, things seemed to be on an upward trajectory. We resumed our walks and even returned to tennis balls and tugs of war. With our second baby on the way, Leah and I took a trip, and Pharaoh's grandparents came into town to watch him.

When we returned home, the tail that used to whip us in the legs like a rope swayed a little more softly. That night, Pharaoh struggled to get around the house and only wanted to sleep. The next day, we had our sign. He looked us in the eyes and told us it was time. He had given everything to us for almost thirteen years. We stayed home together that day, and I opened the door so he could bathe in the sun like he always loved. When we arrived at the vet's office, we carried him in and said our goodbyes. I thanked him for everything—for the companionship, the love, the humor. I thanked him for being Leah's protector. Through tears, I signed the paper confirming we had to let our best friend go.

I have a picture of my son petting Pharaoh on his last day. Hank told him he was a good boy. I cannot look at that picture. What I can do is remember the joy that dogs bring us. I can remember the countless personality traits Pharaoh expressed without saying a word. I can think I hear those nails clicking through my house when it is too quiet. I can try my best to answer when Hank asks me where Pharaoh is. I can cope by writing about a simple yet perfect dog.

ANDREW LEIPOLD lives in Decatur, Georgia, with his wife, Leah, and their two kids, Hank and Hattie. Andrew currently works as a higher education attorney and previously served as an officer in the United States Army. Andrew has always been a dog lover and hopes this essay about his dog connects with readers who have also lost their steady companion.

What a Difference a Little Doggie Can Make

SHARON SUNKLE

MOMMY, MOMMY, WE WANT A doggie!" This was a constant mantra I heard from my three little boys for months. We had just moved into a new home in a new city and had begun to feel settled. I finally felt ready to bring a puppy into our family.

I began praying for a special dog for our family of five, which consisted of my husband Jerry, our three little boys, and me. We wanted a dog that would fit into our family's lifestyle and be good for all of us. Adopting a dog into our family and home was a really big deal. So, I prayed for just the right dog. God knew exactly the perfect dog for us and led me to her.

I called a veterinarian I knew in our town and asked if he knew of a dog we might adopt. I explained I was looking for a medium-sized pup with a calm nature. He said he did actually know about a dog that might be a good fit for our family. A woman had brought in a puppy she was fostering for shots and a health check-up. I called this woman and asked if we could come and see this puppy. She was elated that we were interested.

The little doggy came to us as a half-puppy/half-adult dog after a young couple had failed to train her properly. They both worked full-time and had shut her in the bathroom all day while they were gone, then were mad when she scratched up the door. Thankfully, they decided to give her away to a temporary home, where she was properly house-trained. Our family went to see her at this home, and the minute we walked in the door, I thought perhaps this was the dog for us! She came running to greet us with a wagging tail, floppy ears, and happy eyes.

> She came running to greet us with a wagging tail, floppy ears, and happy eyes.

We went home to really think about it and give it some prayer, which was our habit about major decisions. A few days later, with the decision made, I drove to pick her up. She lay next to me with her little head on my leg as I drove home. Her little body trembled, as she wasn't enjoying the car ride. She never did learn to like car rides, unlike many dogs. We bonded immediately as I spoke quietly to her and petted her little head all the way to her new home.

The boys were so elated to finally have a dog. But they couldn't decide on a name, so Jerry made the choice. Her name was Corkey; don't ask me why. This little doggie had been rejected and was truly ready to give us her love and devotion. And our three boys were thrilled to return to her their own love. Corkey was a curious, fun, and lovable ball of energy. She mostly resembled a Cocker Spaniel with a little Retriever thrown in. She had a beautiful golden coat, big dark brown eyes, a long fan tail, and stood about fourteen inches high.

Corkey had the perfect temperament for our family—laid back and calm. With three energetic little boys, we didn't need extra noise and commotion from a dog. The only time she would bark was when the doorbell rang. And then it was a "Hey, let's see who's at the door" kind of bark, and not the "Get off my porch or I'll bite your leg" kind of bark.

I think God gave Corkey a special ability to sense when one of us needed extra attention. That's when she would jump up into our laps and allow us to pet her and love on her with more intensity because of our own problems or anxieties. It was always calming and soothing to stroke her sweet little head and her extra-soft coat. I've heard it said that petting a dog will actually lower a person's blood pressure! I'm a believer.

When Corkey was about two years old, Jerry was diagnosed with cancer. It was not a good prognosis. He was only thirty-eight years old. Our little family was in a state of total devastation. As his disease progressed, Jerry spent more time in his favorite chair in our family room. And Corkey spent more and more time in Jerry's lap, nudging his hands to pet her. She knew Jerry needed extra comfort and attention. She sensed something was very wrong, and in the only way she could, she helped Jerry by becoming his constant companion.

> Corkey spent more and more time in Jerry's lap, nudging his hands to pet her.

It seemed as though being with Jerry became her mission. She was a young dog with lots of energy, and I think she would have preferred to be out in the yard playing with the boys. However, perhaps Corkey knew that this mission would be short-lived, and she would have the opportunity to play at a later time. That little doggie would follow Jerry all around the house, and the minute she had the opportunity, she jumped into his lap. It was so sweet to see the two of them napping together in Jerry's favorite chair.

Thanks to the wonderful hospice organization, we were able to keep Jerry at home during his illness, except for his chemotherapy treatments. We obtained a hospital bed, which we placed in our family room for the final month of Jerry's life. The bed was too high for Corkey to jump up on, so she would dutifully sit at the side of the bed until someone picked her up and placed her next to Jerry so that she could comfort him.

When the end for Jerry finally came, there was Corkey, waiting and watching with the rest of us. She definitely knew something was very wrong. We had placed Jerry back in his favorite chair, and after he breathed his last breath, we were waiting for the ambulance to come and take his body to the funeral home. As I looked down, there was Corkey, watching my agonizing cries. Then, to my utter amazement, she walked over to Jerry's chair and jumped right up into his lap, gently laid down, and nudged his hand to pet her. She didn't understand this would never happen again.

> Don't ever think that dogs don't grieve; they do.

Don't ever think that dogs don't grieve; they do. Corkey mourned right along with the rest of us. She moped around looking for Jerry, not eating well and being downright pitiful as she lay in the corner with her head down on her paws. Her mood reflected the way we all felt, just plain heartsick. We were actually thankful that Jerry's ordeal was over for him since we knew he was in heaven and he was no longer in any pain. And we knew we would see him again! But the hole he left in our home, in our family, and in our hearts was overwhelming.

Slowly, Corkey began to realize she had a new mission in life. She could sense which one of us needed her the most at the time and offered up her love and devotion to that person. She would entertain us with her playfulness, jump up on our laps, follow us around, and generally keep company with whichever one of us was the saddest at the time. Corkey was such a blessing during this most tragic and sad time. I was dealing with tremendous grief myself, but I was very concerned for my three little boys, ages thirteen, eleven, and five. Children process grief very differently from adults, and Corkey provided a much-needed diversion for us at different times.

Years later, after the boys grew up and went off to college, Corkey became more my dog than theirs. She and I shared many walks and quiet moments together. She lived a good, long life. Corkey left us many years ago, but her memory remains strong as a special doggie God placed in our home for a season. What a difference she made in our home! God used her to give my family comfort and love when we needed it the very most. Her love and devotion will live on in our hearts and memories forever. Don't ever question what a difference a little doggie can make!

SHARON SUNKLE is the author of the book *I Will Mentor You.* Her second book, *99 Thoughtful Thoughts on Life,* will soon be published. Sharon has written articles for numerous outlets and has been a speaker at several women's events. She has led Bible Studies for thirty years and has been a mentor for almost that long. She and her husband, Richard, live in Southern California. They have three sons, two daughters-in-law, and eight grandchildren.

Sammi's Fur-ever Home

MARCIA OKERLUND

A S DIRECTOR OF A SMALL canine rescue in western New York, I've been somewhat unconventional in my efforts to convince a lost dog that I am their friend. I've sat in the woods during a downpour, feeding ham to two pit bulls who'd placed second in a battle with a porcupine. I've crawled under old buildings and through piles of brush. A lost dog can show up at any time in any place. Such was the case of Sammi.

One day, a call came from a couple who discovered a coonhound had intended to make *their* home *her* home. They fed her, and their two Mastiffs befriended her, but this gal kept her distance from humans. Catching her was crucial, as she was clearly pregnant. We needed to prevent her from giving birth in the woods, where finding the pups would be difficult.

Meet Sammi

After assuring the homeowners we would catch the dog, she made it clear our plans differed. My first step was my usual approach for tracking the lost and loose—a large pan of chicken. There's a technique for catching a frightened dog: attract the nose, then the stomach, and finally capture the heart.

I arrived the next day to find the long-legged, floppy-eared coonhound feeling at home. She ran around the yard as if she had always been there. Sammi, as I dubbed her, watched curiously as I tossed chicken her way, but my attempts to draw her close backfired. She remained just out of reach. This might be a battle of wits. The bowl was soon empty, and I had gained nothing. Oh well, tomorrow was another day!

> She ran around the yard as if she had always been there.

The next day, I found Sammi where I'd left her—in charge of the home she'd claimed. This time, she acknowledged me when I called but stood frozen until I tossed out some treats. She accepted any amount of chicken, but only on her terms. Her resolve matched the distance between us, and her determination equaled mine. As I placed each piece of chicken closer to me, I noticed Sammi's incredible ability to stretch to reach it while maintaining a safe distance. Any slight movement on my part, and she ran.

Sammi Remains Elusive

On day three, Sammi waited as I drove up. She seemed excited, but I knew it was what I had affectionately named "The Chicken Van" that attracted her. I sat in the open van, still as possible, holding out chicken, hoping to entice her to come closer. She approached, but not too close.

When I arrived on day four, my long-legged, floppy-eared friend eagerly ran to greet The Chicken Van. She knew she had a good thing going. Finally, she felt safe enough to take the chicken from my hand. This continued for days.

Then I had the brilliant idea that if I could entice her with a piece of her tasty treat while also holding a loop leash, I might just win this battle of wills. For several days, I offered the treat through the loop, growing confident as she moved closer. Trust shattered when I accidentally dropped the leash on her, ending that tactic. She never approached the leash again.

> My long-legged, floppy-eared friend eagerly ran to greet The Chicken Van.

Weeks had passed, and with fall nearing, we feared Sammi would head to the woods to give birth. We needed a plan to move her to a safe place and protect her pups. You've heard the quote, "It takes a village . . ." right? Well, that's what it took to create a plan of action that brought success.

When the homeowners discovered Sammi enjoyed cozying up with the Mastiffs in their doghouse, a plan was born. Leaving a crate nearby, the owners waited for an opportunity. Spotting the dogs together, they pushed the crate in front of the doghouse, crawled in, and successfully moved Sammi inside. Dejected, she was taken to the shelter and given our best room.

Sammi's Birth Experience

Capturing her was timely because the next morning, signs of labor began. Twenty-four hours later, I walked into her room to find Sammi curled up in the corner, looking terrified. She was staring at a blob on the floor—puppy number one. Initially indifferent, the terrified mom showed little interest in her newborn pup. Fortunately, she eventually warmed up and began caring for it. I remained by her side for hours as seven more puppies were born. Despite Sammi's guarded expression, our bond seemed to deepen through the birth experience, suggesting a growing trust between us.

The next day, I learned this wasn't true as I entered her cage to clean. As I switched dirty blankets for clean ones and moved the puppies, Sammi suddenly latched onto my face. A dog's post-birth hormones can be as intense as a human's, and I had met my match with Mama dog! Though I didn't blame her, I did need to explain why one side of my face had turned purple by the time I arrived home.

A New Day, a New Dilemma

Each day, Sammi presented us with new challenges to overcome. After showing little interest in her litter, she was now protective of her pups, and once again, we needed to crack the code that would allow us to handle and clean her pups. Somehow, Sammi had to be moved from her cage to outside to allow us access to her pups. With an eight-foot-long stick with a hook, we devised a new plan.

Using the stick, we successfully unlatched one door after another to open and then closed the doors behind her as she made her way to the outdoor pen. The stick became a point of contention with Sammi, who seemed reluctant to accept help despite receiving fresh blankets and care. After latching onto my finger for yet another bite, it was unclear who would ultimately be in charge—Sammi or me.

> It was unclear who would ultimately be in charge—Sammi or me.

As the weeks passed, we started holding Sammi's puppies up to the window, showing her we could be trusted with them. Over time, she grew comfortable with us in the kennel, allowing us to open the door to the outside pen. She would quickly dart past us, clearly indicating her preference not to be touched. After eight weeks, Sammi's healthy, playful puppies were ready for their for-ever homes.

Treats and Trust

The next challenge for Sammi would be preparing her for her own forever home. The prospect of this happening seemed rather bleak, so we were also prepared in case she needed to stay with us for a long time. The process of building trust began in small steps. First, she was moved into the main kennel to observe interactions between the other dogs and volunteers. She started running freely into the yards when her gate was left open.

> Eventually, she began to tolerate ear rubs or petting. Although, I wouldn't say she liked them.

When it was time for Sammi to return to her kennel, it always happened on Sammi's schedule. Volunteers hid behind every open door, closing them before she could change her mind and wander back out. Eventually, she began to tolerate ear rubs or petting. Although, I wouldn't say she liked them.

Our next step was to get a leash on her. I think she found them humiliating, but with a leash, Sammi could go for walks like the other dogs. Sammi wore a look that made us believe she was always planning an escape that would take her back to the freedom she once had. One night, she succeeded when she pulled the leash out of the volunteer's hand. Freedom!

After receiving the call about her escape, I gathered whatever meat was in my refrigerator, grabbed a few McDonald's hamburger patties, and the dogfight began. Who would outsmart whom? I needed to get her close enough to grab the leash she still wore.

Returning to what had worked before, I sat on the ground, tossing out her treats. It was past midnight before I finally caught her and returned the well-fed coonhound to her kennel. A few weeks later, she slipped out again—this time backing out of her collar and making a run for it without a leash to catch her. Another attempt to capture Sammi found me crawling on my hands and knees with no success. Finally, I managed to open the gate, but the closer I walked toward it, the farther away she went. Once again, a row of treats saved the day!

A Harness and Houdini

The safest way to handle this mischievous dog was with a harness. We added it to her wardrobe and began walking her with two leashes. This method worked well until one cold night when she somehow managed to slip out of both her collar and harness, happily making her way into the surrounding grape vineyard. On that cold winter's night, she outwitted a volunteer once more. Our little Houdini had struck again.

It seemed Sammi had a memory like an elephant, making it harder to lure her with treats. This time, despite enjoying the tasty morsels I left along the trail to the kennel, she refused to enter when she reached the door. I lost count of how many times I refilled the trail, even making another trip to McDonald's. Finally, at 3:00 a.m., I called a truce and gave up. When I returned at 7:00 a.m., Sammi was waiting at the door. She had decided it was time to come in from the cold and enjoy the comfort of her bed and blanket all on her own.

A Fur-ever Home

Sammi continued to be a favorite at the shelter. Who could not love this gal with so much determination to do her own thing? We had become convinced Sammi would remain our shelter dog when we received an application from a veterinarian who had a coonhound identical to Sammi. They were a perfect match for our girl. When it was time for Sammi to leave, there were many mixed emotions among the volunteers.

As we loaded her into the car, the dog who never wanted to be ours looked pleadingly at us with her big brown eyes. We were happy that she found her forever home, but she tempted us to change our minds with her sad eyes. We had all become extremely attached to her. However, this was also the day we had worked so hard to achieve for her.

> This was the day we had worked so hard to achieve for her.

Sammi's new mom assured us that she would keep in touch, and she did. We were overjoyed when we received a picture of Sammi curled up with her brother on Mom's bed. We knew Sammi had indeed found her forever home.

My time with Sammi taught me valuable lessons: perseverance, determination, and thoughtful consideration. Sammi could have spared herself much trouble by trusting sooner. Aren't we often the same? We fear the unknown and fight for what we believe is right, only to find something far better awaits just around the corner.

MARCIA OKERLUND grew up on a farm in western New York with her best friends, Jinx, Snooks, Phillippe, and her horse, Moonshine. Always one to rescue the stray or injured, Marcia has nursed baby birds, an opossum, and a squirrel named Bonkers. She's been a volunteer at the Northern Chautauqua Canine Rescue for over twenty years and served eleven years as the director.

A Paw-fect Pedigree

JOAN M. BORTON

"BILL, EITHER SHE GOES, OR the dog goes. Tomorrow!" Those were the words my exasperated mom sighed to my dad when I was three years old. Earlier that year, King had joined our home. I think Dad was the one who found him and brought him home as a puppy. Mom, who'd had a dog as a kid, knew the work entailed in owning one—no pun intended. Dad called him a "Heinz 57 dog" because King had a little of everything in him.[1]

Dad rigged a cable from the back porch of our house to a tree at the other end of the half-acre property. When King wanted to go outside, Mom or Dad stepped on the back porch and hooked the chain to our dog's collar. King spent hours racing the length of the yard. When he needed to rest, he lay contentedly in the grass, watching whatever was happening in the backyard. When a bunny crossed the lawn, he raced after it, stopping only when he got to the end of his cable. Whenever anyone neared the back porch, he was the first to greet them with barks and sniffs. King took the roles of investigator and protector.

---

1. A version of this chapter first appeared at Word Weavers International. Joan Borton, "Summers with My King," *Word Weavers International* (blog), August 5, 2021, https://word-weavers.com/blog/537-Summers-with-My-King.

For my parents, the protection factor was priceless. But as a young child, I didn't understand. Inside, King and I stayed in different rooms. He scared me, especially when I came in and out of the house. I was becoming proficient at steps, but when he nuzzled me on the outside stairs, which had no railing, I screamed and cried.

> He scared me, especially when I came in and out of the house.

Poor Mom worried I would get my feet caught in his chain or get knocked off the porch onto the concrete walkway. She often had her hands full carrying in groceries and managing my six-year-old sister's entry into the house too. To keep our family safe and things moving, Mom decided to carry me up and down the steps. In the heat of summer, humidity reigned supreme in our part of central New Jersey. Carrying a healthy three-year-old, who went in and out of the house several times a day, became too much. That was when my overwhelmed mom uttered those words that changed my life.

"Bill, tomorrow, either she goes, or the dog goes!"

I'll never forget this statement, in part because it is an oft repeated family story.

I overheard Mom's words as I changed into my nightgown. I wondered, *Am I going tomorrow, or is King?*

My family never showed me I did not belong. I was certain, though, that with the two choices she offered Dad, I must be the one to go. *But where would I go and why?*

This was in the early 1960s, before we became a society that took every word out of context. Neither of my parents ever did anything abusive or neglectful. Mom simply was a tired and worn-out homemaker needing refreshment and a change of pace.

I had a few minutes to think before Mom and Dad came to tuck me in bed and say prayers. As Mom entered my room, I blurted out,

"Tomorrow, when I wake up, I'm going to play with King!" We didn't talk anymore about it, at least not that I remember.

I awoke early the following morning and found King. I showed him my desire to be friends by petting his dark brown and black coat while hugging him around his neck. He rolled over and taught me to rub his belly. His rear paw thumped up and down in genuine delight. When King went outside to run, I ran alongside him. That day, we became fast friends.

Shortly after that, a sturdy railing adorned the steps and porch. I never heard Mom and Dad talk about either of us leaving again.

> One of King's favorite places to hang out was near my feet under the kitchen table.

One of King's favorite places to hang out was near my feet under the kitchen table. When I did not enjoy some part of our dinner, I'd slip it under the table to him. I'm certain this was not as secretive of a move as I thought. Still, I was never reprimanded for it. The rest of the family served him table scraps by putting them in his food bowl.

A FEW YEARS LATER, THE role of protector flipped.

Thick brush grew on the back of our property where King's cable ended. Other than poison ivy, I didn't know what grew back there. But I had no desire to explore and find out. It was easy to obey my parents' words to stay out of that area. Occasionally, I heard Dad mention a plant with an unfamiliar name growing amid the weeds.

Uncle Henry, whom I didn't know well, had come over. He was Dad's older brother. On this summer day, he arrived with a giant sharp blade attached to a wooden handle. I later learned this was called a machine. He talked to Mom and Dad for a while and then walked to the back of our property.

"NOOOOOO!" I screamed and ran out of our home and across our yard to my grandmom's house. Once inside, I hid in the closet in her middle room. Gram found me and asked what happened.

"Uncle Henry is going to kill King!" I sobbed.

Mom joined Grandmom as they explained that Uncle Henry was there to gather rhubarb, the plant Dad noted growing in the back of the yard. He would use the machete to remove some of the brush and cut down the vegetable. He'd take the rhubarb home to Aunt Jean, who would use it to make a yummy pie.

I cautiously peeked out the window. Uncle Henry wasn't in view, but I spotted King running back and forth in the yard. *He's alive!* My little heart and mind were relieved. Still, to be on the safe side, I stayed inside Grandmom's house until Uncle Henry completed his task and the coast was clear. Then, I returned home to resume playing with my best friend—King.

AS I GREW OLDER, MY responsibility for King's care increased. Especially when his long hair shed. Mom kept a clean house, which was important to Dad. As much as he enjoyed King, Dad did not want to see dog hair. I recall vacuuming just before Dad was due home from work. On other days, I sat with King on those same back porch steps, brushing his thick coat. He patiently stayed seated while I stroked his fur and then set aside the clumps of hair. Sometimes the wind picked up the light balls of hair. As they somersaulted across the yard, I imagined they would become part of a bird's nest.

Once every few months, King practiced his best Houdini impersonation and slipped out of his collar. While he explored the neighborhood, I knocked on doors and asked, "Have you seen King?"

I called his name between houses as I walked up and down the street. Sometimes I found him. Occasionally, a neighbor called to tell us King had come for a visit. Other times, he came home on his own after traveling or when he was hungry.

WHEN I WENT OFF TO college, King welcomed me home on school breaks. At least he did for Thanksgiving and Christmas. Over spring break, I visited my sister at her college. On our first day together, she told me the sad news from which Mom and Dad had shielded while I was taking final exams. King, who was now riddled with arthritis and sometimes walked in a horseshoe shape, had taken his final breath.

Decades later, treasured memories of King flood my mind whenever I see a bottle of Heinz 57 sauce or eat a piece of rhubarb pie. As an adult, I've had other dogs as pets, but none can ever compare to growing up together with my King. He had the "paw-fect" pedigree for a best friend.

JOAN BORTON lives in Central Florida with her husband, Jerry. She is an active member of Word Weavers International and WordGirls. Joan most often writes about strengthening families affected by disability. She recently published *MarriageAbility: Embracing the Richness of a Marriage Affected by Disability.* When faced with down time, she will be found swimming, reading in her hammock, or working on a jigsaw puzzle. You can follow her at Luke14Exchange.org/blog or JoanBorton.com.

Those Eyes

TERRIE HELLARD-BROWN

W E ALL LOVE PUPPY DOG eyes. Even cat people love puppy dog eyes. And, sure enough, when we went to get our very first puppy for our children, the eyes had us. Those eyes—those piercing brown eyes.

We have four children. We were missionaries at the time, living in Taiwan, and we told our kids repeatedly, "We can't have pets. Who would take care of them when we go back to the States for a month each year? It's not fair to a pet to leave them for so long."

> Those eyes—those piercing brown eyes.

We stuck to our decision until we knew we were probably not going to be able to go home each year, and we learned that having pets can often help autistic children. Of our four, three are on the spectrum. The desire for a little calmness and helping them learn some responsibility outweighed our other concerns. My husband, Dave, and I talked about it, prayed about it, and went on a secret mission to see if we could rescue a puppy. We would surprise the kids if we found a puppy. Plus, if we took them with us, we'd come home with at least four puppies instead of one.

At the Shelter

We went to the shelter, searching for our rescue puppy, and we went through the whole facility and looked at all the dogs. Several were jumping up on the front of the cage with the "Pick me!" attitude. So many adorable dogs! So many noisy, hyper dogs. I swear the Disney movie was right—they were all calling out to us, "Pick me! Pick me! Pick me!"

We chose one to take for a walk and spend some time with him. He begged us to take him. However, as soon as we got him out of his kennel, he no longer cared if we were even there. His "Pick me!" turned into "I'm free!" as he ran amuck in the park-like play area. He only wanted out of the kennel. He was hyper and uncontrollable. He was not our puppy.

We looked at other puppies. We needed one that could handle four children and the chaos that sometimes happens in a home with kids. We needed a pet that was not overly hyper, scaring our kids. It was a lot to ask for in a new puppy, but we were sure we'd find one.

Those Eyes

We were near the end of the last row of kennels when we saw her. Those brown eyes looked up at me and into my soul. My heart melted. This one sat quietly in a cage with five other hyper dogs vying for our attention. She just rested there in an empty dog dish. Her eyes were pleading, "Take me home." She wasn't nervous about the other dogs but appeared resigned to the noise and chaos surrounding her. I told my husband, "We've found our puppy."

All the way home, she sat in a box on my lap, looking at me with those big, brown eyes full of questions and uncertainty, but she seemed at peace. The pup was sick, and we had to give her medicine. She was malnourished, so we knew we truly rescued her from the brink of death.

When we got home, we surprised the kids. I swear she looked at me with horrified eyes, as if haunted by memories of the five dogs running around in her kennel, sure she was walking into the same situation with our four kids. But soon, they quieted down and gently petted her. She relaxed. She was home.

> This was the most gentle, regal dog I've ever seen.

She came to life within a day or two, and we had a new member in our family. This was the most gentle, regal dog I've ever seen. We named her Ginger because of her brindle coat that had flecks of ginger color throughout. We often commented on how she sat as if she thought she was a princess. Yet, Ginger could get the zoomies better than any dog, jump higher than we could ever imagine, and make the hound dog bark like a champ. She was a mystery and a blessing all rolled into one.

A Surprise

About a month later, our younger daughter came home with a surprise. "Mom, someone dumped a whole box of puppies on the road! This one crawled out of the box and almost got run over. I couldn't let her get run over! Can't we keep her?"

Dad immediately responded with a no, but I took the puppy that literally fit in my hand and had her nuzzling my neck as I talked to her. I was hooked. Dave had no hope. Four kids and his wife begging to keep the puppy was too much, and he agreed. This little puppy was too young and wasn't weaned yet. She had that skunky puppy breath. We took her to the vet and fed her milk until she was old enough for food. The vet assured us she would not get very big.

The size of the dogs was important. We lived in Taiwan. On the twenty-fifth floor of a high-rise. Big dogs and small apartments don't mix. However, we learned that sometimes vets lie. The puppy grew from the size of my hand to forty pounds that year. She was black, so of course, we named her Pepper. We now had the Spice Girls, as we called them, and our family was complete.

> We now had the Spice Girls, as we called them.

Ginger, the regal, quiet one, now had a sister who was a bundle of energy and orneriness. Pepper was rarely quiet, her black eyes dancing with energy and ready for fun. When Ginger was sometimes overwhelmed, she would hide under our bamboo couch for respite. We kept the dogs' leashes on because we were training them to go outside (twenty-five stories down) to do their business. Keeping the leashes on gave us a fighting chance of getting them out in time. However, this also gave Pepper the opportunity to pull her sister out from under the couch to play. Ginger was not amused, but we were impressed by Pepper's determination.

Third Culture Dogs

Both dogs were Formosan Mountain Dogs (Taiwan Dogs). So, even though they weren't literally sisters, they were the same type of dog, which is a breed that is no longer thoroughbred. Early on, the species was mixed with Portuguese Greyhounds. Our dogs definitely showed those qualities. They could run like the wind and easily jump over five feet. They were perfect. God had really answered our prayers. Our children learned to be responsible with their dogs, and they helped calm our children. Both dogs had so much personality, and they blessed our family more than we could have expected.

Several years later, we prepared to move back to the USA. We jumped through all the hoops to bring the Spice Girls with us. Twelve hours in a kennel in a cargo hold does not sound like my idea of a fun way to travel, but both girls did great, and they learned to love their adopted country. In fact, they soon discovered the most amazing thing ever: SQUIRRELS!

Our backyard had an abundance of squirrels. The dogs had never seen squirrels, but they immediately began chasing them, guarding our yard from these intruders. The squirrels would taunt them at times, and the war was on! The dogs never caught one, but they kept them away from our yard. In fact, Pepper made sure they knew she meant business. We got her a toy squirrel, and one day, she took it outside. I watched her, wondering what in the world she was doing. She went right out into the middle of the backyard, put the toy squirrel down, and looked up into the trees. Then she picked up the toy squirrel and shook it from side to side violently. She dropped it (like a mic drop), and she looked up into the trees again. If she could have done the two-finger "I'm watching you" gesture, I'm sure she would have. She was a true American dog now.

Both dogs guarded our house well. They stood on the back of the couch barking at the mail carrier, the neighbors walking their dogs, and any visitors who came to the door. I don't know what they would have done if we'd truly had an intruder, but they were doing their due diligence in this new home.

A Long Good Life

We rescued these two dogs, and they blessed our family beyond measure. They were healthy and happy, and they helped us and our kids feel healthier and happier than we were before they joined our family. As they grew older, our vet was always amazed at how healthy both were. But then we hit a sudden turn. Pepper began to decline quickly. She had cataracts and doggie dementia, which affected her back leg. Even with cloudy eyes, she would look into my face with sadness. I responded, "I know. Getting old sucks." I would pet her and tell her how much we loved her. One day, not long after she began to decline, she got out of the backyard, and no one saw her again. After a month of searching, we knew in our hearts that she was gone.

Ginger stopped eating. We thought she was grieving for her sister. We took her to the vet. We gave her medicine. She still would not eat and was wasting away. At a return vet visit, they found tumors. We had to let her go. She was suffering, and those beautiful brown eyes were once again pleading with us. Now, they seemed to be saying, "Let me go." With much prayer and heavy hearts, we let her go.

> We rescued them, and then we let them go.

We had both dogs for just under fifteen years. We rescued them, and then we let them go. Now, we hold on to the joy and memories for the treasures they are. We know God brought us all together, and we felt a strong sense that he walked with each of our girls as they left this life. I don't know if dogs go to heaven, but I know we will never forget what they have brought to our lives. We will never forget the zoomies, the personality, and those beautiful eyes.

TERRIE HELLARD-BROWN is a writer, speaker, podcaster, wife, mom, and a Christian trying to live her faith daily. Her books include *Building Character through Picture Books: 25 Family Devotions Based on Favorite Picture Books* and *A World of Pancakes,* a picture book. Her writing appears in *Starlight Magazine, Upper Room,* and *Inspire Christian Writers.* She speaks at homeschool conferences and women's events and is a member of AWSA and other professional organizations. terriehellardbrown.com

Which Pet?

MAUREEN MILLER

It matters not that Dog is big,
Nor that his teeth are large;
Cat thinks that she is royalty.
Yes, she's the one in charge.

Perched on a chair like it's her throne,
She oversees it all,
Then flicks her tail and cleans her face
With one pink-padded paw.

She has no fear when back is turned
Away from furry beast,
'Cause Cat believes, in order and rank,
Dogs, of course, are least.

It's felines who rule, dogs who drool—
Of this, who wouldn't know?
To them, she'd say with haughty voice,
"Yes, Cat is the star of the show!"

Then with a bow of her tiny head
She resumes to lick her bib;
But with a sigh, Dog shuts his ears
To feline's prideful fib.

For he knows the truth, though won't make a peep,
Allowing Cat to conclude,
Over canines they reign (though he thinks her insane!)
And to him, she is very rude.

But because he is peaceful, humble to boot,
Dog rests his weary eyes,
Dreaming of walks and bones and balls,
And again, he smacks and sighs.

To him, it's not needed to argue or boast
To clear up confusion or fog,
'Cause if it were he who had to pick,
he'd certainly choose a dog.

But the question remains: What would *you* choose
If you could pick a pet?
A furry friend is a special thing—
All gifts from God, heaven-sent!

MAUREEN MILLER is an award-winning author who contributes to *Guideposts* as well as several online devotion sites. She loves collaborative work and has stories and essays in more than twenty compilations to date. Enjoying life in all its forms, Maureen lives on a hobby homestead nestled in the mountains of western North Carolina with her husband, Bill, and their three children and grandchildren. She loves to share God's extraordinary character discovered in the ordinary things of life. www.penningpansies.com

Lady of the House

LISA-ANNE WOOLDRIDGE

"WOULD YOU LOOK AT THAT?" I stood before my desk, taking in the view that would now be mine. We'd just moved in, and I'd claimed my spot—the window faced a beautifully landscaped neighbor's yard, complete with a waterfall of small pink roses cascading over the fence. It seemed ideal since I'd be sitting there most days working on a novel. If I couldn't find inspiration looking at what could pass for botanical gardens, there was no hope for me.

As I tried to take it all in, a small calico cat crept out of the heavy brush, climbed the fence, and perched on the gate. She peered into the window at me as if she was looking for someone. I try not to anthropomorphize animals unless I'm doing it professionally, but I could have sworn she wore an expression of both desperation and hope. She made eye contact with me, and after a few seconds, she jumped down and hurried away.

A Heartbreaking Cry

A few weeks later, I'd settled into my regular routine of work in the morning before things got too busy. The open window let in the warm, scented breeze, enticing me to daydream as I tried to write the next scene in a chapter. My reverie was interrupted by a cry so sad that I called my husband to go outside immediately and rescue whatever it was. My own cat, Muse, leaped up to the windowsill and stood staring down at the ground. She turned to me and gave a mournful mewl, unlike anything I'd heard from her before. Somehow, I understood. The cat outside had cried out in grief. My own cat responded with what could only be called pity.

My husband, an unrepentant animal lover, raced back into the house and grabbed a bag of treats, a water dish, and a can of cat food before dashing right back out. I was happy to let him handle the situation. Babies and animals instinctively trust him. A few minutes later, I peeked out and saw him sitting on our patio, hand-feeding a malnourished, rough-looking cat. It was the same calico who'd jumped up to peer at me through the window when we'd first arrived. After a few bites, she curled up next to him on the seat and fell fast asleep. He looked at me through the glass door and shrugged as if to say, "I don't think I can move." Something about how she was sleeping made me think it was the first time she'd felt safe in a long time.

> After a few bites, she curled up next to him on the seat and fell fast asleep.

For a few days, we fed her on the patio, giving her water and tuna and the priciest cat food the grocery store had to offer. Hey, don't judge. My husband takes his "Best Pet Dad" T-shirts very seriously. She never moved from the patio furniture except to eat or disappear over the fence for a few minutes to relieve herself. Otherwise, she sat exactly where she first sat with my husband. Each of the kids took turns going out to visit with her, and I did as well. She was so affectionate with each of us but also very wary if anyone made an unexpected movement or sound. I told Andrew, my husband, that she looked as if she'd been through the wars. I estimated from her condition that she was a senior cat and resolved to make her remaining time, however short or long, as comfortable as possible. Everyone agreed, including our other pets, who visited with her through the screen door.

> The trouble was, though, she didn't belong to us.

A Mystery Solved

The trouble was, though, she didn't belong to us. That, and we'd only ever had indoor cats. I wasn't sure she'd want to live exclusively inside. So, we set out to see if we could find out who she belonged to. She wasn't chipped and didn't belong to the neighbors we'd met so far. The house next to us, with the beautiful park-like yard, seemed to be uninhabited until late one afternoon when a woman came by to water the flowers. My husband went out to say hello and introduce himself. We hoped she'd know about the status of the sweet little cat we were all becoming attached to.

After a long chat, he came home and relayed the story. A year before, the former owner of our new home had passed away, leaving behind her beloved calico cat. She was an elderly lady who lived alone, and the cat was her whole world. The daughter who inherited the house just threw the cat out to fend for herself. The neighbors, who were only there part time to care for the garden, felt sorry for the cat and had tried to help by putting out food once or twice a week for her. The poor little thing had cried a lot at first but eventually settled in the bushes and seemed depressed.

After just over a year of deprivation, freezing nights, and cold, rainy days with no one to give her love, she must have seen the activity as we moved in. No wonder she'd jumped up onto the fence to peek in the window. She was hoping her lady had returned. She must have been so confused when she saw me, not her sweet, older lady. The cry I'd heard from my window sure sounded like despair.

The neighbors were delighted that we wanted her and relieved that she would no longer have to fight off the neighborhood wildlife or try to stay warm in brutal weather. She was still showing signs of exhaustion, sleeping round the clock on our patio, but she was eating well and purring loudly for each family member who stopped to visit with her. She was a little more standoffish with me, though, but I thought I might know why. Once we had the green light, I stepped out on the patio, sat beside her, and had a little chat.

A Heart to Heart

"Pretty girl, I know things have been really hard for you, and you don't understand where your lady has gone or why you were thrown out and left alone. But I want you to know that lady loved you, and I think she'd want us to love you too. This was your home first, and I know you miss her. But if you'll let me, I'll try to love you as much as she did. She wouldn't like to see you scared or cold or without a lap to sleep in."

She raised her head and regarded me with her bright green eyes as if she understood. A slow rumble started in her chest, and a moment later, she laid her head on my knee to rest. I stroked her head a few times and watched as she visibly relaxed.

"Right, you're going to need a name. And a bath. And a trip to the veterinarian unless we can find one who makes house calls. Sorry about that. But in the end, it'll be worth it. I promise to love you and scritch your ears and keep you in catnip. I know I can't take her place, but this house needs you. You'll have to be the lady of the house now."

She scooted closer and curled around me, seemingly content with the petting and my soft tone.

"So, how about Belle? I don't know what your name was before, but Belle suits you because you're such a beauty. How about it, Belle? Would you like to come inside?" She stood up and stretched and looked at me expectantly, so I stood up too.

> "Welcome home, Belle. You'll never have to leave again."

"Are you ready to come home?" I pulled the sliding glass door open and waited. The kids had tried to entice her inside previously, but she'd stood her ground and refused. Now, she leaped to the stair by the door, sniffed the air, and stepped over the threshold. "Welcome home, Belle. You'll never have to leave again."

A Happily Ever After

It's been two years since Belle decided to take a chance on us. She gradually lost her wariness and regained her health. The vet told us that she wasn't a senior cat after all; she'd just been in such bad shape it seemed so. She transformed before our eyes—her fur is soft and shiny, and she's filled out exactly right. She's lived up to her name by becoming a beautiful cat. She's asleep right now on my son's bed, and it warms my heart to know she's not outside fighting for her life. She seems grateful, too. Whenever one of us goes to check on her, she grabs our hands and lays her head in our palms, purring. She loves to rest on us. It's as if the relief is palpable.

She eventually stopped searching the house for her lady, but sometimes, she still lets out a sad little meow before landing on my shoulder for cuddles. I understand. I'm sitting where her lady sat, so I open my arms, and she settles in. I tell her how much her lady loved her and how good she was for keeping the lady company. I tell her that her lady has gone ahead of us and isn't alone any longer. I tell her she did a wonderful job and maybe I'll write stories for children about her one day. I think Belle would say everyone needs to know it's OK to take another chance and that God sees the lonely ones and gives them families to love. I'd say what an incredible housewarming gift she is, my little lady of the house!

LISA-ANNE WOOLDRIDGE is inspired by illuminated manuscripts and stained-glass windows. Her heartwarming true stories have been published in several popular collections. Her second novel, *The Cozy Cat Bookstore Mysteries—The Rose and Crown*, is now available online. She lives in the land of mountains and valleys that drink in the rain of heaven—otherwise known as Oregon, or you may find her at www.Lisa-Anne.net.

Pawprints in Time

BECKI FULTON

GREW UP LOVING ANIMALS, AND from my earliest memories, they have always been a big part of my life. My dad bred and raised Siberian Huskies, and when I was about four, I was given a kitten. My grandpa also kept his ponies on our property when I was very young. When I was four and a half, we moved with a few of the Huskies and the cat to a dairy farm in central Wisconsin, where I could be around animals whenever I wanted.

I loved to follow my dad around the barn. He would park me in the calf pen, where I cuddled little Holsteins and let them lick my chin until it was raw. I made sure every calf and cow in the barn had a name because, to me, every four-legged creature deserved one. But dogs have always held a special place in my heart. I have a few favorite photos of a Husky puppy licking my toes and one of me pulling our giant male Husky, Chico, in a little red wagon.

Sadly, I lost that kitten early in our time on the farm. However, when I was about seven, my parents surprised us with a Pomeranian Poodle mix they found as a "giveaway" (now we say "rehomed"). They went out one night, and when they came home later, Dad was carrying a scraggly pup in his arms. She had matted fur and desperately needed a bath. I'm sure she was meant for the whole family, but I always called her *mine*! Buffy was the perfect size for dressing up in doll clothes and became my best friend.

Later, after the Huskies were gone, my dad had a Border Collie, Lacy, who was the smartest dog I've ever known. She had a special connection with the cows and took her farm chore of rounding them up for milking very seriously.

AS A CHILD, I DIDN'T completely comprehend all that it meant to be a dog owner. My childhood memories were filled with the fun of having pets, but as an adult, I have had to face the full reality of a pet's lifespan.

> My childhood memories were filled with the fun of having pets.

Now, I must confess that, yes, I am that pet parent who humanizes her pets more than I probably should, but they've always been members of the family! I call myself and my husband Mommy and Daddy, and my human son has always been Brother. Before anyone rolls their eyes, I also know reality and that they are pets. However, the hardest reality of it all is how short their lives really are—a fact that was completely lost on me when I was younger. When Buffy and Lacy left us, I was eighteen and twenty-one. Life was busy then for several reasons—college, careers, moving, and a parent's illness. So, while I was sad when our beloved dogs passed, life kept moving on, and so did I. But as an adult, the loss of two pets over the last six years has been much different for me.

Macy was our first anniversary present to each other in August of 2003. My husband, who grew up with Scottish Terriers, wanted to find a Scottie puppy. He found an ad in the newspaper online for a Scottish Terrier/Shih Tzu mix, and we drove three hours to see her. She was four pounds and oh-so adorable, and we fell in love immediately. We had to wait a bit before she could come home with us, giving us time to prepare before returning to pick up our little bundle of joy.

> She was four pounds and oh-so adorable.

Well, we learned a lot in the first days, for sure! We discovered what she should eat, how to keep her quiet at night, and how to keep her from attaching herself to my son's pant leg as soon as he came out of his room. At her first vet visit, we were told we had two of the most stubborn breeds in one dog, and she lived into that to the very end. So stubborn! Macy would walk away when told no, only to do whatever she wanted when our backs were turned.

Macy looked more like a Schnauzer than either of her breeds, so she had much longer legs and could jump up or down from almost everything. I can still see the scratches on our back patio door where she would "Tigger" jump up and down to let us know she was ready to come inside.

I could share countless stories of this girl and everything she taught me over the years, but it was in her final days and passing that I learned the most. Macy was just over fourteen when we found out she had congestive heart failure. Though she was her feisty self until about this time, we noticed some changes—she slowed down, breathed heavier, and lost weight despite eating like she always had. She still did her daily "perimeter check," as we called it, to ensure our little backyard was safe (she taught this to two younger sisters, who continued to do the same).

I kept asking the vet, "How will I know when it's time?"

She always responded, "You'll know."

The vet prepared us for how Macy would change. Then, one day, two months shy of turning fifteen, her condition literally changed overnight. She wouldn't settle. She paced the house all night, started a little dry cough, and picked at her food. My son and I took her to the vet, who confirmed it was time.

We took her home to have one more night. We made a memory paw print. She said goodbye to her beloved "Papa" (my father-in-law). She snuggled with us. I had given my son the option if he wanted to go with me through it all, and despite never experiencing this kind of loss before, he chose to stay by my side. I'm grateful for that.

We shared beautiful moments with our girl, my son took some very precious photos, and we said our goodbyes. It took a *very* long time for us to leave the parking lot the next morning and head home without her. But the one thing that gave us the greatest comfort was remembering how well we loved her and how well she loved us!

That thought has comforted us each time one of our girls has had a health scare. We love them while we have them because their lives are very short. But they have an immense impact in that short time.

MACY HAD BEEN AN ONLY dog for a few years until I found her "sister," MacKenzie, on a website out of Ohio. MacKenzie was our first purebred Scottish Terrier. She embodied the breed in pretty much every way (I'll let you google to understand that fully). Macy was an amazing trainer despite my lack of knowledge when we'd trained her. Together, Macy and MacKenzie taught us about unconditional love. MacKenzie—who was curiously interested in "screen time" and even enjoyed full-length movies—left us in July of 2023, four months shy of her *sixteenth* birthday. We were told when she was five that she had bladder cancer and had an estimated one to one and a half years to live. That was when we adopted the motto of "love them while we have them" and practiced remembering how much we had loved them and how much they loved us. I'm sure you've done the math and can see she lived well beyond that prediction. We now know she most likely didn't have the cancer they thought she did, but rather a growth or polyp.

> We adopted the motto of "love them while we have them."

MacKenzie was almost completely deaf and had a vestibular issue in the last few years leading up to her final days. Two months before her passing, we found she had congestive heart failure. We had thought we'd have more time with her after she had rallied a bit on a new medication, but ultimately, Kennie (our nickname for her) left us in true Kennie fashion—in her time, on her terms. She just laid down and went to sleep after an early morning perimeter check. We hadn't called her a diva all these years for nothing—it was always her way!

OUR GRIEF DIDN'T LOOK TOO different for either of these girls. And the joy their lives brought to us was also the same. Everyone grieves and honors those who have passed differently—in the human world and in the pet world. We chose to keep the cremains of both of our girls in exquisitely carved wooden boxes that we have with their memorial paw prints, and we treasure the memories and photos we have collected over the years. And the two live on through the three Scottie-girls we currently have.

Like MacKenzie, Fiona was trained by Macy eight years ago. Most wouldn't recommend bringing in a puppy with a twelve-year-old dog, but Macy took on her little sister without a single issue! Macy, MacKenzie, and Fiona were a trio for a little while.

Maddie joined us six years ago when we decided to start looking for a puppy and found out that she was born the day our Macy passed away. And Hazel—the youngest—was born the day after MacKenzie passed, so we knew she was meant to be ours as well.

I know there is much speculation about whether pets and animals go to heaven when they leave us. I will not be able to know the answer to that, but I do know that God created them, and he created us to care for them. And maybe they bring a little bit of heaven to us on earth. I've been blessed beyond measure in the pet department, and I'm happy to be their "pawrent" and for the girls to be my "pawters." Each pawprint in time is an impression on our hearts.

BECKI FULTON was born and raised in Wisconsin and moved to California after marrying her husband, Dave, in 2002. She has one adult human son, Nate, and five fur-daughters, Macy, MacKenzie, Fiona, Maddie, and Hazel. She's also "grandma" to two grand-cats, Ahsoka and Leia. She has been an administrative assistant most of her career, currently at a local high school. She loves being part of worship for her local church, visiting with the ever-growing family in Wisconsin, and trips to Disneyland.

Freedom Restored

SUE FERGUSON

WITH MY HUSBAND'S RETIREMENT ON the horizon, Randy and I decided to leave our larger city home and move to a little house in the north Georgia Mountains. We live on a one-lane, dead-end road in a forest community. It's simple and peaceful living—a little piece of heaven. At least, that's what I thought until my hubby began to travel often for work. Our little house amid the trees seemed too quiet and isolated when he was gone—almost eerie.

After Titus, our chocolate Labrador, died, Randy had said, "No more dogs." I understood and agreed. Life was easier.

But home alone, in the middle of nowhere, made me reconsider. A four-legged friend sounded like the perfect solution to those silent, lonely evenings. Eventually, Randy decided a dog would be a nice addition too.

With our children grown, it seemed to be the perfect opportunity to put my energy into training and molding a puppy into the perfect dog. As my obsessive personality kicked in, I read books, listened to podcasts, and took an online course to set my future pup up for success.

My excitement grew with each possibility. If we had a trained therapy dog in retirement, we could potentially assist in schools, hospitals, and care facilities. What a great time of my life to contribute to those outside of my family. I was committed to the purposeful, fun-filled task ahead.

> I was committed to the purposeful, fun-filled task ahead.

Three months later, Randy and I picked up our carefully selected cream-colored puppy. We'd agreed on a Goldendoodle, and I gladly went along with Randy's name selection for our pup. After all, the fluff on the top of his head did resemble his namesake: Einstein. And I hoped he would be smart and love to train. With confidence, I looked forward to a fabulous partnership.

It didn't take long for my thoughts to fall out of dreamland and return to reality. This pup didn't act like the perfect little pups I'd watched on the training videos. If I had a treat, Einstein lost his mind with delight. He bounced into the air and began a series of enthusiastic pirouettes.

Einstein's super-sized food drive meant his training treats had to be eliminated. After all, his focus needed to be on me. Once treats were removed, that problem was solved; he stuck to me like Velcro. If I stood at the kitchen sink, he napped on my feet. Wherever I moved, he followed. The only thing he liked better than me was food. Hubby called him a walking belly. We limited his food to mealtimes.

In my attempt to socialize him, and because I'd read that he shouldn't be left alone more hours than he was months old, I took him with me for appointments. He enjoyed resting during my haircut and watching when the chiropractor adjusted my back. We walked around the big box tool store and visited our prospective groomer—with him in my arms. We even dropped by a high-end specialty pet store. When home, he met some neighbors and their new puppy. Einstein bobbed and wriggled with excitement through each adventure.

Nights were rough. His crate was in the master bedroom. He hated it. Trying to keep Randy from buyer's remorse, I slept on the hardwood floor beside Einstein's crate. Because of that less-than-comfy situation and taking him outside in the middle of the night, I was exhausted.

This season is short. Things will get better soon. Comforting myself helped, but not for long.

The situation worsened. Einstein no longer complained about the crate; he was too sick to cry. Not only was he throwing up, but he had the runs—and in my attempts to continue his potty training—he had me running outside several times throughout those dark, cold, wintry nights.

> One night was especially bad; I'd never seen a dog so sick.

The vet gave him fluids and sent us home. Einstein's symptoms continued. My energy was zapped. One night was especially bad; I'd never seen a dog so sick. Early that morning, I cried as I texted photos of my pup to the vet. Randy left for the airport shortly before the vet instructed me to take Einstein to the animal hospital as soon as possible.

Weary and frightened, with Einstein in a crate in the passenger seat beside me, I headed toward Atlanta.

The diagnosis was Parvo. The outcome uncertain.

"We will call you every day with an update on his condition and any increases to your bill; you need to pay half today. Bleach the crate, floors, and everything he's touched in your house. Throw out his toys and bedding. Spray bleach in the yard and remove any leaves or debris where he's been."

Overwhelmed with sadness, I followed the instructions. The housework was a lot, but the yard work was daunting. I persevered, moving wheelbarrow loads of leaves and sticks day after day. If my eleven-week-old puppy came home, I wanted him to have a clean and safe environment.

Five days later, Randy flew home, and we were able to pick Einstein up at the hospital. When the doctor brought him to us, he squealed with delight and leaped out of the doctor's arms and into mine. *He remembers us.*

> He squealed with delight and leaped out of the doctor's arms and into mine.

Happy and amazed that Einstein was fine, we drove home. Our frightening ordeal was over, or so we thought.

Before long, we noticed that Einstein was in a severe state of anxiety when we returned home from brief outings. The floor of his crate was askew, and his chin was wet. We set up a camera so we could watch him on a phone when we left the house. The picture was not pretty. He cried and bit at his crate, desperately trying to escape. I was afraid he would hurt himself. We couldn't leave him in that much stress.

There were two contributing factors to his separation anxiety—one was my fault, and the other was caused by his hospital stay. My mistake was that I hadn't yet learned that developing emotional and mental strength in a puppy is important. I'd focused on bonding him to me and unintentionally avoided assisting him in building toughness and confidence. I needed to teach him to be secure in his crate, alone for a little while each day. Of course, I couldn't have known what he would face in ICU. Because he was contagious, he had been crated in isolation. While necessary, it must have been torture for my Velcro puppy.

I couldn't undo either of those past experiences and was helpless as to how to deal with our unfortunate results. Neither my husband nor I felt comfortable leaving Einstein home alone during this stressful time. I consulted a separation anxiety specialist. Her fee—for the months she anticipated it would take to overcome this issue—was more than the whopping bill from his five days of intensive care. Everything I read instructed you to take baby steps out of your house each day, slightly increasing the number of steps, for weeks. The situation seemed hopeless.

Finally, after interviewing several trainers, we signed up for weekly private classes. The trainer told us basic obedience would build Einstein's confidence and likely reduce his anxiety. In the meantime, only one of us could leave the house at a time. Hubby and I couldn't go anywhere together. We were miserable.

Fortunately, we weren't upset with each other. But we both hated the situation, and we couldn't foresee it ending anytime soon. Our freedom was gone.

In the meantime, Einstein, the most joy-filled puppy I've ever observed, happily ran like lightning through the woods and excelled at basic obedience. He was fine as long as one of us was home. We were not.

> As we all know but often forget, seasons change.

But, as we all know but often forget, seasons change. Einstein did gain confidence. A friend suggested we try leaving him without crating him. I'd never let our previous dogs have free reign of the house when they were only a few months old, but we began to take walks and watch him on a phone app. Then we drove around the neighborhood, watching his every move. He was fine. We began to resume going places together—always keeping an eye on my phone and what the camera revealed.

Most people who met Einstein said he was the best trained dog they'd ever seen. My future with a therapy dog was scratched though. Einstein is way too happy and exuberant for that role; we should have named him Pogo or Tigger.

The real test came on the Fourth of July. Our community hosts an annual fireworks display. The grandkids that live nearby came up for it. All of us went, leaving Einstein at the house by himself.

I watched my phone instead of the fireworks. Einstein paced the floor a bit, but most of the time, he rested against the front door, calmly waiting for us to return. That night, I knew we were survivors. Einstein home alone *and fine* while fireworks blasted was confirmation of his maturity and our renewed independence.

SUE FERGUSON lives in the North Georgia mountains with Randy, her husband of forty-five years, and Goldendoodles Einstein and Wilson. The doodles compelled Sue to a greater understanding of following one's Master; watch for her book, *Doodle Desperation*, coming in 2025. In the summer, Sue loves hanging out with her fourteen grandchildren and their parents—preferably at the lake on paddle boards and kayaks. www.thesueferguson.com

My Favorite Walks, by Higgins Wilbanks

KIM WILBANKS

FOR MOST OF MY LIFE, the routine was the same. The first thing every morning, my human would take the red leather leash off the hook, attach it to my collar, and off we would go. We walked in my neighborhood, at the beach, in the mountains, and any other place we might go. I loved going for walks. It was the highlight of my day.[2]

Walking the Neighborhood

Mahm opens the screen door, and we head out across the backyard. Sometimes I can smell "the girls" walking down the fairway of the golf course before we even see them. As soon as I take care of my business, we head west on Golf Lane. We walk to the corner, then turn left on Lone Palm Drive. I usually make several stops to smell the smells along the way. Koya's mahm calls

2. This chapter first appeared on Kim's blog. Kim Wilbanks, "My Favorite Walks by Higgins Wilbanks," *Feathering My Empty Next* (blog), October 20, 2019, https://kimwilbanks.com/2019/10/20/my-favorite-walks-by-higgins-wilbanks.

it "checking our pee-mail." Mondays are always a good day to walk because of all the additional smells and greetings from the nice sanitation workers.

It's always fun to run into my friends when we're on a walk. Sometimes, I see Sassy and Jaxy from down the street. They're nice even if they are a little Frou Frou. I always enjoy visiting with Koya while our humans stop to talk. That new youngster, Shelby, is always excited to see us. She can be a little rambunctious, but, after all, she is still a puppy. I miss seeing some of my old friends like Roxie, Molly, Max, Kaylee, and Neula.

We always walk to Mom-Mom and Dad-Dad's house in the cul-de-sac. If they are at home, we go in and visit for a while. I especially enjoy lying in front of the fireplace on cold winter mornings. Mom-Mom gives me more treats than Mahm. Unfortunately, I gained so much weight that she had to give me green beans. That's OK, though—as I like to say, "Food is food." After a brief rest, we walk back to our house, where I nap the rest of the day.

As I like to say, "Food is food."

When I was a young pup, we went for longer walks—sometimes on the golf course. I loved it when Mahm would take my leash off and let me run like the wind. Of course, she would check for alligators first. Mom-Mom used to walk with us when she was a young pup too.

Walking the Beach

We take the elevator down to the first floor. (I used to go down the stairs before it got hard on my back.) I poke around the tiny yard while Mahm puts on her shoes. We go through the gate and cross the street to get to the sidewalk. I take care of my business, and then we head south.

We walk a couple of blocks before we cross the street. There is an old white house on the corner. No one lives there now. It is where they have community plays. Mahm has to drag me away from the playhouse because I could spend hours smelling all the smells. It's also where the meanest cat used to live. I knew he lived there because I could smell him even if I couldn't see him. One time, I was minding my own business, sniffing the bushes, when he jumped out at me, hissing and flailing his paws. He scared me half to death!

A few years ago, our walk would vary from this point. I had three or four different routes I would take—maybe down Pine Street or Magnolia, then cut over to North Shore, then back up Coconut to our house. All of that changed two years ago when I made the most marvelous discovery.

One day, we passed the playhouse and walked to the cafe on Magnolia. (It always smelled so good—like bacon.) We crossed the street and walked on the road that ran parallel to the beach. We turned onto the sidewalk in front of the beach houses standing like sentinels facing out to sea—my favorite place to walk. It was pleasant because it ran between the row of houses and the beach, and there were no cars. We walked a couple of blocks and stopped in front of a brand-new home. It was a big gray house with an iron gate. Outside the gate, the people set out a bowl of fresh water and a big container of treats for us dogs. Jackpot!

Ever since we discovered the house with the treats, it's the *only* way I want to walk. Sometimes, we walk all the way to the big house and there are no treats, which is most disappointing. When the people are home and the treats are out, Mahm lets me have *one*. I have been known to circle the block to pass by the gray house in the other direction, hoping to snag another one, but she doesn't fall for that trick.

Another great thing about walking on the island is the group of nice men who drive the golf carts around, doing work for the city. They carry treats for us dogs. It confuses me that *all* the golf carts don't carry treats. There should be a law about that.

I'm not allowed to walk *on* the beach. That's OK, though. One time, I went to a doggie beach and drank too much salt water. I got sick and had to spend the night in the emergency veterinarian clinic. I did not like that.

I got to feel the sand on my paws a few times. My humans liked to walk to the bay on Easter Sunday morning to watch the sunrise. They'd let me sit beside them on the sand as we watched the sky begin to glow and brighten. It was kind of like a reverse sunset.

Walking the Mountains

I'm kind of like my humans—I like the beach *and* the mountains. Please don't make me choose. When we are in the mountains, my favorite place to walk is the city park.

We ride in the Jeep to get to the park. I like riding in the Jeep, especially when the windows are down. We usually walk around the big circle first. Sometimes, children are playing soccer in the field. I want to play with the balls too. There is an old barn, and Mahm always makes me stop to take a picture. (She takes too many pictures.)

> Mahm always makes me stop to take a picture. (She takes too many pictures.)

We pass the dog corral and the playground and get to my favorite spot—the stream. I love to get in the cold water even though it feels icy. Mahm doesn't get her feet wet, but the other human, Jim, walks to the middle of the stream with me. Sometimes, he throws rocks to splash me. One time, there were two other Corgis at the park, and we had a little Corgi party in the middle of the stream.

Sometimes, we go for a ride in the mountains and have a picnic. We explore the trails that are easy for me with my short legs. One time, when we went for a walk on a trail after a picnic, an enormous snake blocked our path. Yikes! That was scary!

> I enjoy crunching sounds—makes me think of treats.

It's always nice to walk in the mountains, especially when it's cool. There is nothing like a walk in the brisk mountain air with a jewel-toned backdrop of fall leaves. They make the best crunching sound as we're walking. I enjoy crunching sounds—makes me think of treats.

The Last Walk

One day, when I wasn't feeling well at all, my humans took me to the vet. It was strange because Mahm usually took me by herself. I didn't mind going to the vet. The people were pretty nice, and they gave me Cheez Whiz. I love Cheez Whiz. The lady at the front desk took us to a quiet room with soft lights. I sniffed around, wondering when they were going to break out the Cheez Whiz. My humans kept staring at me, and their eyes were wet. *Hmmmm,* I wondered, *What's up with that?*

One of the nice humans at the vet came and gave me a little shot. Ouch! I looked around the room again and yawned. I thought, *Maybe I'll just lie down and take a little nap.* I glanced up at my humans, and they patted my head. Mahm held my paw. This time, I let her.

When I awoke from my nap, I felt so different, so refreshed. I yawned and stretched. *That's weird—my joints don't ache,* I thought.

I licked my chops, but I didn't feel that annoying growth in my mouth anymore. It was gone! I jumped up—*What's going on? I thought I was in a quiet room when I fell asleep, not in this beautiful green meadow.* Something caught my attention, and I glanced behind me and watched a rainbow-colored bridge fade away.

The sound of barking in the distance caught my attention. It was a familiar little yipping. *Wait, is it? Could it be?* A little Yorkie came running toward me and threw all his weight on me in a body slam. Max! My old buddy Max! I hadn't seen him in years. We tumbled over each other, playfully growling, our tails wagging. Then a couple of Pugs came running over—my first girlfriend, Roxie, and her sister, Molly. My cousins Sophie, Shadow, and Mudje ran up to greet me, followed by "the girls" who used to live a few houses down from me. They all crowded around me, licking, barking, and wagging their tails. "Come on," they said. "We'll show you around."

I started off after them but paused for a few seconds and looked back toward the vanished bridge. I sensed something I could not see—a deep, deep love. Someone beyond the haze loved me, and I knew it. I wasn't sad but felt great joy. I blinked my eyes against the fading memory, turned, and ran off to be with my friends. This was my forever home.

KIM WILBANKS is a wife and mom with two grown, married children and two grandsons. She and her husband of forty years are life-long residents of Florida who enjoy spending time at the beach and the mountains of North Carolina. Kim enjoys reading, crafting, jigsaw puzzles, travel, history, and her Labradoodle, Boone. She is a believer who enjoys Bible studies and mission trips. You can find her writing about empty nest life at www.kimwilbanks.com.

Comfort and Support

Trust Your Guide

LISA J. RADCLIFF

I T WAS MY DREAM JOB, and it was mine! After a few years as a volunteer, raising puppies for The Seeing Eye, Inc., I was hired as a puppy development area coordinator. My job consisted of placing seven-week-old puppies in volunteer homes (fairy godmother-like), training the families to raise the puppy to become a successful guide, addressing any behavior issues, and finally, returning the puppy to headquarters when it was time for their formal training (some would say Cruella-like). Basically, I visited families and played with the puppies they were raising, like a puppy social worker. It was incredibly fun, rewarding, and I got to meet some amazing people—all while participating in the Seeing Eye's mission of enhancing the independence and self-confidence of people who are blind.

As part of my new job training, I spent one day as if I was blind. It was called orientation and mobility training. I went through that day at the Seeing Eye headquarters under a blindfold. It was something I was excited about and terrified of doing. The best part of the day was working with a Seeing Eye® dog who had just about completed its training. While I wasn't good at eating meals blindfolded (relieved everyone at my table was also spilling things), I could hardly wait to take hold of that harness and have a dog guide me through the streets of Morristown, New Jersey.

> I could hardly wait to take hold of that harness and have a dog guide me through the streets.

I had a definite advantage over a lot of the students in my class. They were college students who were learning about orientation and mobility as part of their college classes. For most of them, it was their first exposure to working with guide dogs. But I already knew how the dogs were trained: to stop for or go around obstacles, stop at curbs and stairs, watch for traffic, and stay away from drop-offs like the ones on train platforms. They learn that they are as wide as their body and their person together and as tall as their person. I knew the commands to use and all the nuances of following the dog's lead. But my work was with the puppies, getting them ready to go into formal training. I had seen dozens of Seeing Eye dogs working with the trainers as well as the blind students who lived on campus for several weeks, learning to work as a team with their dog. But now it was my turn.

I was matched with a little yellow Lab. We greeted each other with anticipation for a great day together. She was wiggly and energetic. It's important that we have a good rapport because these dogs don't work for treat rewards. They do their job because they love the person they are working for. Her trainer was there with me, so she would work well just because he was there, but I still needed to initiate that relationship with her. That was easy enough. As I knelt to give her some ear scratches and tell her how beautiful she was, I was bathed in puppy kisses. I was used to that at work, but she was all business when I picked up her harness handle. She was eager to get going, and so was I. We took off, with her trainer walking behind us, keeping a watchful eye (more on me than on her—she knew what she was doing).

People who use guide dogs tend to walk fast, and now I knew why. In this bustling little city, it felt as though there was nothing around me. I didn't need to watch out for anything. As far as I was concerned, there was nothing in my way, nothing to distract me; I could just go. It was exhilarating. What amazed me most was when the trainer would say something like, "She just took you around someone waiting for the bus. She moved you to the right to avoid a trash can at the curb." I couldn't even tell; to me, it felt as though we were moving in a straight line the whole time. I followed her lead without any hesitancy because I knew I could trust her.

I knew I could trust her.

"Trust your dog" is a phrase often spoken by trainers to their students. It's the most important part of becoming a successful team. Trust is one reason The Seeing Eye, Inc. only accepts people with a significant level of blindness as students. If a person can see, they may not trust the dog, even though the dog is trained to keep the person safe. If they don't completely trust the dog, they will second guess the dog's decisions and not work together as a team. They may think their way is clear, but they don't see small obstacles or cracks in sidewalks or something in their periphery. The dog sees all of that and makes adjustments to avoid them and keep the person from harm. So, by not trusting their dog, they may walk right into trouble.

I thought of the phrase often as we breezed down the sidewalk. Sometimes, I was unaware of small corrections the dog made to our course. Other times, as it's trained to do, the dog would stop and wait while I felt with my foot to determine what was blocking our way or if we had come to a curb. Then I would give the dog the "forward" command, and it was up to the dog to determine the best option and guide me in that way. My job was to trust the dog.

Perhaps the biggest test of trusting my dog was crossing the street. As taught, I listened for the traffic, and when I thought it was moving next to me and not in front of me, I gave the dog the "forward" command. Now, it was up to her to decide if it was truly safe. She could see what I could not. Was there a car turning into our path? Was there a hybrid car or a bicycle coming that I couldn't hear? Was someone running a red light? Would I trust the dog's judgment when she started to cross, even if I thought it wasn't safe?

> I kept thinking, "Just trust her. She can see what's going on and will keep us safe."

The Seeing Eye calls that process intelligent disobedience. The dog needs to disobey the "forward" command if it will put us in danger. But once the danger has passed, the dog will then proceed. I felt the pull on the harness and stepped into the street. Hearing cars and not knowing where they were was a little unnerving, but I kept thinking, "Just trust her. She can see what's going on and will keep us safe." And she did!

When we got across the street, she stopped at the curb so I would know I needed to step up. I praised her for doing such a good job and was rewarded with a wagging tail beating against my leg and a little extra speed in our pace.

As a Christian, I saw so many parallels of trust to my walk with God. I wonder how often he corrects my path without my noticing, keeping me from harm. How often does he point out a danger and wait for me to trust him to guide me around it? In his sovereignty, he safely guides me along the narrow way that leads to life. And he does it because of his great love for me.

Too often, I burst headlong through life without asking God for his guidance. I stumble in the darkness and wonder how I got so lost along my way. Or I think I see a clear path ahead of me, unaware of the obstacles and pitfalls lurking. But he is always right there by my side, ready to take the lead, not just guiding me but also protecting me. Even when he directs my path through unnerving places, I have nothing to fear. All I have to do is trust him.

LISA J. RADCLIFF is an author and speaker in southeastern Pennsylvania. Lisa has been a homeschool mom, a puppy development coordinator at The Seeing Eye, Inc., and now writes and speaks full-time. Her most recent book, *A Time To Laugh: My Life Over Fifty*, highlights the joys of this season of life, especially the funny things grandchildren say. To reach Lisa, visit her website at www.lisajradcliff.com.

Dolly and John: A Love Story

GAIL SCOATES

T HE PHONE RANG IN THE other room as I was cleaning. I dropped
what was in my hands and ran to answer before they hung up.
The phone identified the caller, and I felt a moan come from
deep within me.*

"Hello?"

"Hi, Gail, it's Nancy from the Hospice House. You sound like
you're busy, but I wonder if you and Dolly might be able to come
and visit John. I just left his room, and his daughter followed me
out. He's close to death, and she thinks Dolly's presence might help
make this transition a bit easier."

Dolly was my thirteen-year-old Golden Retriever and therapy
dog. We were one of the volunteer teams that stopped by every
week to see the patients and families. The nurses had told me Dolly
was his favorite therapy dog, so John's room became a special stop
on our rounds.

"As you know, he's been declining for the past few weeks, but
I think this time, the end will come soon," Nancy told me. His
daughter, Carole, and others were visiting, and she thought all of
them could benefit from seeing Dolly.

My voice cracked, and my heart was broken as I replied, "Sure. We'll be there in about an hour. Just need to change and get ready." Although I wasn't surprised to receive this news, tears formed as I thought about John's life coming to an end.

I had been a hospice nurse for many years. In that role, getting a call from a family member of someone I was caring for was common. I often tried to amend my schedule so I could be with them when their loved one died. It was one of the gifts I felt a call to give. Sometimes, things would go very fast, and other times, the end lingered for a long time—only God knew this final chapter of their life. I knew hospice from a professional point of view, and I also knew it from a personal view. While it is heart-wrenching, it can also be a time of beauty and peace.

> While it is heart-wrenching, it can also be a time of beauty and peace.

I squatted down, took Dolly's face in my hands, and looked deep into her eyes.

"Oh, Dolly, what an honor to be asked to share this special time with John and Carole. It means that all the time we've spent with John was meaningful not only for him, but Carole and the nurses also appreciate our efforts." I patted her head, and we began the task of getting ready to see our friend.

Even though today was going to be different from our regular "workday," we still went about our usual routine. A good brushing was followed by a thorough cleansing with doggie wipes. Then on to brushing her teeth (Dolly's favorite part), putting on her collar reserved just for work, and finally, her official volunteer nametag. She was an old hand at her job as a therapy dog and seemed to understand that these grooming steps were part of the bigger picture.

While we prepared for today's special visit, I reflected on John and the times we had spent with him. It usually started with, "Where have you been? It's been weeks since I saw you last." He said this almost every time we visited, even though we'd been there just the week before.

We would arrive at the Hospice House and hear from the staff, "Dolly's best buddy is waiting for her, so you'd better get in there." Sometimes, our stop with John lasted so long that Dolly had only an ounce of energy left to see the rest of the patients and families. I felt guilty, but he loved seeing Dolly, and I had a hard time cutting our stay short.

Most of the times we visited, he was sitting up in a chair with one of his books. John loved dogs and had dog pictures around the room. He was also an avid reader. When we arrived and he'd hold up a book, I knew we were in for a detailed synopsis of his favorite parts of the book. Now and again, he'd save a magazine for us because there was a dog on the cover. "This one reminded me of Dolly," he'd say.

John was quite a character and liked to tell stories of the many adventures of his ninety-plus years of life. He had worked in marketing, traveled all over the United States, and worked for a time as a radio disc jockey. He liked to brag about his occasional major league baseball game broadcasts.

> Dolly loved nothing more than someone to give her their full attention and a good massage.

Occasionally, I'd hear him drop a few well-known names. "Did you ever hear of Al Capone? Well, I met his brother-in-law one time when I was out in Las Vegas, and . . ." I never knew if the stories were true or not, but I enjoyed hearing him tell his tales. "Do you ever listen to WJVD? I was on that radio station from time to time, and I interviewed . . ." and on he would go.

As John talked, he would often have Dolly sit between his legs and rub her face and head and speak to her as he reminisced. Dolly was happy to oblige as she loved nothing more than someone to give her their full attention and a good massage. And if he stopped talking or rubbing, she would turn and look at him as if to say, "Don't stop now."

One topic that never failed to be part of our conversations was his dog, Chance. Chance was a small dog that John rescued and had for nearly fourteen years. "Took him right off the street," he told me. John made sure Chance never had a bad day after that. Said he took Chance everywhere he went and never left the dog alone. When he needed to be out of town, Chance simply moved in with his daughter, and then she took him everywhere.

"Do you need to leave already?" was what Dolly and I heard each time we prepared to depart.

"John, there are other people here we need to see today too."

"Ach, they can wait. We aren't done talking yet," was his standard response.

While it was hard to say goodbye, after each visit, my spirits would lift when I heard him pick up the phone, call his daughter, and tell her, "Dolly was just here." The nurses told me he called Carole every time after we stopped by.

Today when Dolly and I arrived at the Hospice House, we signed in as usual. Then we went to the nurses' station.

"Hi, Nancy. We're here and ready to see John."

"Come on with me. As we walk, I'll tell you what's going on."

As we headed to his room, she gave me a few updates. Even though the nurses never gave me confidential information, I appreciated that they respected my background as a hospice nurse.

We walked to his room. Nancy knocked and softly opened the door.

"Hi, everybody. Dolly is here to visit," Nancy spoke softly as we walked in, and she introduced us.

I went over and hugged Carole. We had met a few times before, so I felt comfortable making this contact.

"Carole, I'm so sorry about your dad. Please accept my deepest condolences. He has a very special place in our hearts." I nodded to the others in the room.

I looked at the person lying in the bed, and tears came to my eyes. We had been here only a week ago. Although John was not able to be in the chair the past few weeks, he had been upright in bed with his same silly smile and stories. But not today. Today, he was lying flat on his back; his eyes were closed, and his breathing was shallow.

> John had insisted she be up on the bed and lay next to him.

Even though Dolly was not supposed to be on the bed, for the last few weeks, John had insisted she be up on the bed and lay next to him. He had lost a lot of weight and was only skin and bones, so there was plenty of room. I was careful to make sure Dolly did not step or sit on him. She had fallen asleep alongside him the last time we visited while he petted and patted her, slowly massaging her soft coat.

Carole knew Dolly had lain on the bed next to her dad the last few times we visited, so she asked if we could do the same today. Once I placed Dolly carefully on the bed, Carole asked me to help arrange John's arm around the dog. Dolly was a willing participant. After all, this was her good friend.

We stayed for more than two hours. Dolly seemed to know that this was where she was needed. She slept much of the time but occasionally would open her eyes when people were talking, or someone came or went from the room.

When it was time for us to slip away, Carole started to cry when her father's arm fell softly to the bed without Dolly there to hold it up. She hugged us just before we left.

"You have no idea what it means to me that you and Dolly would come by to see my dad. I'm convinced he was aware that she was here today. He loved dogs, and he loved his little Chance, but he especially loved this dog. He talked about her all the time. I have peace in my heart right now. Thank you for coming today."

Later, the nurses told me that John passed away peacefully in his sleep that night. Carole was with him when he died.

I had given John a copy of my book in his better days, signed with my name and a stamped paw print with *Love, Dolly* written beneath. Carole had asked the nurses to give it back to me the next time Dolly and I came for our volunteer work. Inside was a heartfelt thank you note from Carole placed in the book on the page where I had written Dolly's and my names. John had written on the same page, in almost illegible handwriting, these words: "I love Dolly."

Names changed.

GAIL SCOATES is an award-winning author of *Paws, Purpose, and Possibilities: How Therapy Dogs and Faith Healed My Heart.* With a heart for God and for dogs, her books show us how God's creation can teach about God's love. A retired registered nurse, she also trains and evaluates teams for therapy dog work, writes, and travels. Gail is a member of the Advanced Writers and Speakers Association, Word Weavers, and the Christian Independent Publishing Association. www.pawspurpose.net

Hope Remains

MAUREEN MILLER

"Hope" is the thing with feathers . . .

SUCH BEGINS EMILY DICKINSON'S FAMOUS poem. But honestly, without reading the rest of her words, this opening line used to conjure an image for me of hope being fleeting, something that just might fly away. Disappear.

In fact, while Hope didn't have feathers, she did remain, at least for a season. Even more, love—especially motherly love—was the greatest thing about her, bringing her the most joy.

Hope was a dog—a mutt of sorts, though she certainly had some Spaniel in her DNA. White with a peppering of black spots and a feathery tail, she came to live with us soon after our move to western North Carolina in 2002. Friends of ours needed to rehome Hope. "Might you take her? She'd be the perfect addition to Selah Farm," they said. And she was, sort of.

The problem? We already had a dog, a puppy named Jack. Furthermore, my in-laws, who lived next door, had two dogs. Shadow was a sweet-tempered black Labrador, and Blue Girl, who happened to be our Jack's momma, was a spunky and playful Blue Heeler, not to mention a tad territorial.

And Hope? She didn't quite fit in, at least not at first. After all, dogs can be leery of newcomers, something especially true for Blue Girl concerning the new dog on the farm.

Those two! Blue Girl and Hope sparred over food, fought for attention. They would even fight over where they'd use the bathroom. Like two competitive teenage girls, those dogs! All we knew to do was pray they'd eventually come around.

THINGS DID SETTLE DOWN SOME—that is, when we added yet another dog to our pack, a gentle Golden Retriever puppy our young sons named for the calf in their favorite Christmas movie, *Annabelle's Wish*. The pup's presence drew out nurturing tendencies in Hope, who, at no more than two years old herself, mothered the newbie— sharing the same bed, snuggling with her, and cleaning Annabelle from head to tail.

They were fast friends, which was fine. After all, Jack was closest to his next-door biological mother, and all appeared happy on the home front.

Well, almost.

> In truth, it wasn't the dogs who struggled anymore. It was me.

In truth, it wasn't the dogs who struggled anymore. It was me. Despite my wonderful husband, our two amazing boys, and a loving, close-knit family next door, I battled sadness as I waited for the fulfillment of what I believed were promises from God—words I held dear, knew were from him.

The root of my despair was infertility—barrenness that robbed me of experiencing the joy of carrying a baby in my physical body.

Yes, I loved our boys, and I knew God brought them to our family at just the right time, in just the right manner. Still, I longed to know the pleasure, the sensation, of life inside me—to feel the kick of growing feet, the flutter of movement I'd only heard about from other giddy moms-to-be over more years than I cared to count.

When we moved to our farm in the summer of 2002—the fifty-acre property tucked in a valley, surrounded on all sides by the Smoky Mountains—we'd already suffered the loss of a daughter through a failed adoption. Though my heart had healed considerably, I still held on with hope, desiring for more children to be added to our family. Furthermore, I believed God had biological children for us. Hadn't he said so? Or so I thought.

> I still held on with hope, desiring for more children to be added to our family.

My mom knew my love for children's picture books, and she gave me one several years prior to our move south. A lovely story, it's by children's author Patricia MacLachlan, and we enjoyed it many times while we still lived on that quaint, tree-lined street outside Indianapolis.

"Read *All the Places to Love*," one or other of our boys would exclaim, and we'd snuggle up to read it again, savoring its beautiful illustrations by artist Mike Wimmer.

"Wouldn't it be nice to live somewhere like that?" I'd sigh, pointing to the picture of rolling hills dotted with dancing daisies. "That sure is a place I'd love to call home!"

So, when we found the small farmhouse nestled in the rolling hills of western North Carolina, we thought it too good to be true. It was like stepping into our favorite storybook.

After our move, however, I discovered something more—learning a truth whispered to my heart by the One who loves to give good and precious gifts to his children, no matter their age.

One day, not long after our last box had been unpacked, one of the boys pulled the familiar book from the shelf. "Read this again, Momma," he asked, handing me *All the Places to Love*.

Tucked in among pillows on our bed, I opened it and read—the boys joining me from memory in parts, sometimes aloud, sometimes just their little lips moving.

Suddenly, words struck me in a new way. Though I'd read them countless times before, God had a fresh message for me, a message that also correlated with a passage of scripture I'd only recently learned and had committed to memory. "He gives the childless [barren] woman a family, making her a happy mother" (Psalm 113:9).

In the children's book, the mother and her son climb a hill on their property on a bright blue spring day, each carrying a bucket. They hike up to visit a favorite spot on the farm—the blueberry barrens, where an abundance of blueberries grew.

And I heard his whisper, "You can be fruitful too—yes, even in your barrenness."

Not understanding what a blueberry barren really was, I researched further, learning there are actual places where growth is intentionally burned. The result? An even greater harvest of fruit. Death to life. Destruction leading to fruitfulness.

> I clung to the promise that God could and would use me.

As this truth settled into my heart, I began to walk in greater joy—believing I, too, could be fruitful despite infertility. I clung to the promise that God could and would use me, not merely in spite of but because of my literal barrenness, and this revelation was a game changer.

But there was one more thing—something about that beautiful illustration of mother and son climbing the flower-dotted hill, cirrus clouds swirling upon a cerulean sky. Seeing the picture of them hiking to the blueberry barren, one of our boys pointed it out. "Look, Momma! That dog—it looks just like our Hope!"

And it did. The faithful pup by the mother and child's side in the illustrator's artwork was the exact image of our loving pet—the mutt who, despite some hardship, also found a home on Selah Farm. Though she struggled to find her place at first, Hope embraced the beauty of motherhood after we adopted a pup we named Annabelle.

Indeed. And though our dog had fur rather than feathers, Hope's presence—her faithfulness and love—remained, at least for a season. And God used her to affirm to us that though there are circumstances in life we might not understand, difficult seasons when we can't quite comprehend his ways, we can always, always trust his heart.

And you know what else? I agree with Emily Dickinson. "Hope" is the thing with feathers, helping us soar to all the places—to all the people—God gives us to love.

Even to—yes, even in—blueberry barrens.

MAUREEN MILLER is an award-winning author with stories in more than twenty collaboratives. She contributes to Guideposts' *All God's Creatures*, her local newspaper, and several online devotion sites. Married to her childhood sweetheart, Bill, Maureen enjoys life with her family, including two furry beasts, on Selah Farm, their hobby homestead nestled in the mountains of western North Carolina. She blogs at www. penningpansies.com, and her first book, *Gideon's Book*, will be released in early 2025.

Little Angel

LISA-ANNE WOOLDRIDGE

At the top of the hill, no matter the weather,
my kitten waited to walk home together
in a small town called Providence.
Tucked way back in the trees of Kentucky,
wherever we went, I felt lucky
to have a lovely cat who loved me like that—
I named her Little Angel.

In the woods of Providence, I needed
someone to watch over me—and she,
with the heart of a lioness,
chased a snake away from my tree.
She comforted me when I wept
and stayed with me while I slept,
protecting me even in my dreams,
my sweet, fierce Little Angel.

When I was lost in the dark hollow
miles away all on my own,
she found me in the purple shadows
and called me to follow her home.
I dried my tears in her fur—
while she purred and purred—
my beautiful Little Angel.

A faded photograph proves her existence,
me with a radiant smile in my innocence,
now hidden in a box of childhood treasures.
She kept safe my breaking heart—
helped me when life was falling apart.
For her uncomplicated love, I'll be grateful forever,
my darling Little Angel.

I never knew God had so many ways
to pour out his everlasting love
or that the Voice had such a choice
of eloquent fires lit by so many tongues,
or that by the smallest gift, I would know
a message from the One who loved my soul—
he sent my delightful Little Angel.

For many years, I dreamed of Providence
where I roamed with my sweet girl;
dreamed she went on ahead of me,
to that better world.
I imagined she sits on top of a golden hill
with perfect weather, waiting for me,
so we can walk Home together,
my faithful Little Angel.

There is no more sacred a pet
than one who brings the Father's love—
and there is no more blessed a child yet,
than the one born again from above,
who learns to trust, and to receive
the gifts of God for those who believe,
and treasures like my wonderful Little Angel.

LISA-ANNE WOOLDRIDGE is inspired by illuminated manuscripts and stained-glass windows. Her heartwarming true stories have been published in several popular collections. Her second novel, *The Cozy Cat Bookstore Mysteries—The Rose and Crown*, is now available online. She lives in the land of mountains and valleys that drink in the rain of heaven—otherwise known as Oregon, or you may find her at www.Lisa-Anne.net.

Whimpers and Whiskered Prayers

MELISSA A. MCLAUGHLIN

HANNAH HAS A DIFFICULT QUESTION for you," my dad sputtered through the phone when my husband answered. Our ten-year-old daughter, Hannah, had spent the night with my parents. We grew uneasy at my dad's guarded comment.

"What is it?" my husband inquired, a wary tone in his voice. My husband's brow creased as he turned toward me.

"I'll let Hannah tell you," Dad replied.

"Can I bring a lost kitten home with me?" Hannah quivered. "I found it abandoned and crying in Grammy and Gramps's barn."

> How could we say no to our precious daughter with a tender heart toward animals?

My husband paused. We didn't need another pet. Our household was lively enough with a family of five and our two cats,

Scooter and Nosy. Yet, how could we say no to our precious daughter with a tender heart toward animals?

Even as a toddler, Hannah cupped frogs and caterpillars with awe. She revered the gift of each creature's life. Her love for animals ran deep. We imagined her pleading eyes and longing heart. How could we say no?

Before we could respond, my dad returned to the phone. "I have to warn you about one thing," Dad faltered. "The kitten is so small and wispy that I doubt she will live through the night. We tried feeding her milk on a saucer, but she's too underdeveloped to lap. If she can't drink, she won't make it. Are you sure you want a kitten that probably will not survive?"

Silence.

Finally, we understood the cause of unease in this conversation. We were not talking about a spunky kitten full of life. This kitten was nearing its final breath, too young to be without its mother.

Dad relayed the story to us.

THEY HAD BEEN RELAXING ON the porch that morning when they heard a distressed moan. Dad strained to pick up the faint cry. He and Hannah paused and listened in stillness. There it was again. A pitiful animal's yelp beckoned them.

Together, they followed the squeaky wail. The whimpers led them to the old barn behind my parents' house. They creaked the barn door open, and there she was. A tiny, abandoned kitten with gray fur and sorrowful eyes met their gazes. The kitty appeared to be just a few weeks old. No mother in sight, she rocked toward them on wobbly, newborn legs.

Her mews continued. Hannah reached for the kitten and nestled her close. The creature vibrated in Hannah's arms with contented purrs. My daughter's face glowed. A longtime animal lover, Hannah's eyes sparkled in wonderment.

With the mother cat missing, Hannah's arms cradled the ball of fluff and gently carried her to safety. Hannah dug out a doll blanket and swaddled the kitten like a babe. They offered warm milk from a saucer, but the kitten was not old enough to lap milk.

Dad lifted the kitten for a closer look. Her frail body fit in the palm of his hand. A small spot of blood had dried near her nose. Though very small, the kitten suffered no other injuries. Dad's concern lingered, however. He feared the feline was too young to survive without her mother. It continued its hungry cries, but milk on a saucer was useless for a kitten who could not lap milk.

Next, they tried dipping a handkerchief in the milk to see if the kitten could suck milk from the cloth. They were unsure if this helped, but it was the best they could do. That's when they made the phone call.

Together, we pondered this tenuous situation.

> Together, we pondered this tenuous situation.

In the background, we heard the sweetest plea. "Please, Dad. Please may I bring her home with me? Maybe we can help her."

With two other young children at home, we recognized the potential for tears and broken hearts at a kitten's graveside. Yet, Hannah's heartfelt appeal echoed in our souls. How could we say no to a motherless, vulnerable kitten? How could we say no to Hannah?

My husband and I nodded at each other. With calm assurance, he said, "Yes, Hannah. You may bring the kitten home." We heard Hannah breathe a sigh of relief.

SQUEALS OF DELIGHT BOUNDED THROUGH our house as we informed our two other children that Hannah was bringing a kitty home. We explained the serious nature of the kitten's size, age, and prognosis. Our other daughter and son listened with big eyes and quiet faces, their exuberance tempered by the sobering news.

"We'll take care of the kitten the best we can, but only God knows if she will live," we explained.

After a quick trip to the pet store, we assembled our supplies. On the counter, we spread out the kitten milk and a specially made bottle, a small water dish, and a shallow pan for litter. We arranged the laundry room for our new guest, lining a cardboard box with towels for her bed.

Hannah arrived home with the bundle of fluff wrapped in a doll blanket. Soulful, golden eyes peeked out. Snuggling the kitten in her arms, Hannah slipped to the laundry room and settled the frail pet in the towel-lined box. With soft, gray fur and slender whiskers, the kitten tentatively sniffed around.

We estimated her age to be three or four weeks. Despite our best efforts, the kitten could not lap milk or water from a dish. Next, we tried the bottle. First, I tried. Then Hannah tried. Miraculously, my husband found the right touch. He cuddled the kitten against his chest, and she began to gulp milk from the bottle without coming up for air.

> This was our first glimmer of hope.

This was our first glimmer of hope. If she could consume nourishment, perhaps she would make it through the night. One by one, the kids stroked her downy fur and cooed to her with soothing voices. We whispered prayers, asking God to strengthen her body and keep her alive. Our love enveloped the furry feline as we tucked her into the towel-lined box for the night. We drifted to bed and wondered what tomorrow would bring.

At dawn, the whole family stampeded downstairs. I held my breath. Did we need to dig a grave or buy more kitten milk? Slowly, we cracked open the laundry room door. The fluffy gray kitten opened her eyes and a tiny mew resounded. It was music to our ears.

Cheers rang out, "She's alive! She's alive!" Still teetering, the infant kitten meowed as we warmed her milk and prepared her bottle.

The sun rose in our hearts. Smiles lit up our home. Joyful laughter reverberated. The kitten survived her first night of many more to come. The miracle of life took on new meaning as we treasured another day with this wee, tender kitten.

> The sun rose in our hearts. Smiles lit up our home.

Our son received the esteemed honor of naming the new pet. Our daughters, both older than our son, had chosen names for our other two cats. So, this time, it was his turn. He deliberated long and hard. Finally, he announced his decision with confidence. It was fitting. He named her Lucky.

The homeless kitten was home.

THIS BELOVED MEMORY OF ADOPTING an abandoned kitten reminds me of God's deep love for us as his cherished and sometimes lost children. Wherever we may be, he looks for us when we cry out to him. He never misses the silent tears that fall at night or the private sigh others cannot hear.

God hears and reaches for us. May our hearts, minds, and souls rest in his everlasting arms of love. "The eyes of the LORD watch over those who do right; his ears are open to their cries for help" (Psalm 34:15).

Whether we are dancing on the mountaintop or trudging through life's valleys, God sees, hears, and loves us. Imagine him extending his arms for us, holding us close, and comforting us right where we are, more perfectly than how my husband held that sweet and helpless kitten. We are not alone, for his ears are attentive to our cries. In his arms, we are home.

Names changed to protect privacy.

MELISSA A. MCLAUGHLIN is a teacher, writer, and speaker. After a fulfilling teaching career, Melissa earned a Certificate in Foundations of Biblical Studies and now encourages others through her faith and words. Melissa enjoys taking walks with her family to delight in God's beautiful creation. Cats still grace her home, keeping everyone on schedule with humor, antics, and cuddles. For more information about her books and blog or to connect with Melissa, visit www.melissamclaughlin.

Paws and Pray

BARB SYVERTSON

LOVE PEOPLE WHO LOVE ANIMALS. You won't find a nicer group of folks. Unfortunately, I'm not one of them. As long as I can remember, I've been afraid of all animals, even squirrels. My parents told me that as a young child, a dog bit me. I don't remember it. But that was the beginning of my fear of even the sweetest of dogs. (I also feared curlers in ladies' hair and plaster casts on broken arms. But I digress.) My parents' strategy was to get a dog. This would help me get over my fear. Or my fear of dogs, at least. They were wrong.

Soon, a basset hound puppy we named Cindy joined our family. I do remember thinking she was so cute and small and harmless. But I also remember coming down the stairs each morning and stopping on the step right above the puppy gate. I would call for help. I needed someone to put the tiny beast into another room so I could enter the living room without her jumping on me.

Dog owners typically believe that everyone feels the same way about dogs as they do.

"Oh, she won't hurt you."

"Don't worry; she's friendly."

"Just give her a minute, and she'll leave you alone."

"She likes you and just wants to give you a kiss."

That all sounds like solid pet advice, but it just doesn't help someone like me. Picture this: your friend has a pet snake that roams freely around their house. When you go to visit, the snake greets you at the door and tries to slither up your leg. You sit down on the couch, and the snake climbs up onto the couch and into your lap. She continues to scale up your body toward your face.

The owner says, "Oh, she won't hurt you."

"Don't worry; she's friendly."

"Just give her a minute, and she'll leave you alone."

"She likes you and just wants to give you a kiss."

Does that sound like fun to you? I'm sorry to admit that this is what it feels like to me when I encounter even the friendliest of dogs.

Basset hounds are adorable—perfect for a pet calendar or greeting card. They have the sad eyes and long droopy ears, but the jowls are the starting point for long strands of thick drool. When they drink, their long, floppy ears get wet. Bassets shake their heads to get rid of the glop and the water from the bottom of their ears. I was not a fan of spray drool. Not then. Not now. Call me crazy.

> I was not a fan of spray drool. Not then. Not now. Call me crazy.

My parents hoped I'd come around as I got older. I didn't call for help at the gate anymore, but I still rarely touched her or played with her. I tolerated her. In my teen years, I was the first one home from school, so my job was to let Cindy out into the yard, open a can of dog food, spoon it into her dish, freshen her water, and let her back into the house. I did it for years, but I could never do it without being grossed out by the smell and consistency of the food, gagging every single time I had to scoop it out. To this day, I can't stand to open my husband's favorite canned hash because I still have the same visceral reaction.

Cindy would howl, usually to be let back into the house. She could also sit on her bottom with her torso straight up. We nicknamed her "Fire Hydrant." Her legs were so short that her belly practically dragged on the floor when she walked. She was a couch potato without the benefit of being allowed on the couch.

My sister Joyce was sure that if Cindy was just given a chance to exercise, she would rise to the occasion. So, she arranged for a dog date with the neighbor and her dog. Her friend's dog was perky and energetic and eager for the walk. Cindy wasn't. Halfway around the block, she laid down on the sidewalk and wouldn't get up. No amount of pressure, prodding, or dragging got her to budge. Seemed like she didn't enjoy blind dates. Or maybe she was too out of shape to continue. Joyce had to lift our heavy and uncooperative dog up and carry her home. These are not the stories that make you eager to bring your dog in for Pet Show and Tell at school.

FAST FORWARD A DECADE OR more. I was now married to a man who grew up with a beloved pet dog named Patches. Ed's relationship with his dog could have made a great Hallmark movie. And remember, I might not love animals, but I do love animal lovers. Great people. So, when we had children, he wanted our kids to have a Patches experience. We got a beautiful little black Lab puppy, which we named Nicki (short for Nickelodeon, the kids' favorite TV network.)

Again, I was the first one home in the afternoon, so I re-enacted the routine of my youth, minus the gagging because, thankfully, we used dry dog food. All the dog training was done by Ed. He did a very good job, and everyone loved Nicki. I was ambivalent about the new member of our household. Nicki took a shine to our youngest son, Todd, who was three when the puppy arrived. They were buddies. This was sweet, and even I knew that this dog was digging a place in my heart.

> Even I knew that this dog was digging a place in my heart.

Todd went to preschool a few mornings a week with his cousin Ryan. My brother-in-law shared the transportation duties with me. On a cold day in February, I dropped the boys off at their school and headed home. Ed was home from work that day for President's Day, and we decided, at the spur of the moment, to run an errand during preschool hours. My brother-in-law typically brought them home because the preschool was right near where he worked, and he often went home for lunch.

On our way home from the errand, it started to snow. It was the kind of storm that came quickly and strong. The roads got icy, and visibility was terrible. Although we were going slowly and cautiously, we got trapped on the highway because of a snow-related accident ahead of us. We were stuck. No one was moving for a long time. I watched the clock, and my heart raced. Would we make it back in time for Todd's drop-off?

Wearing just flimsy sneakers and a light jacket, I left the car and my husband parked on the highway while I trudged through the slippery snow to a restaurant along the road. My freezing-cold fingers managed to work well enough to place the call. My brother-in-law didn't answer his work phone or his home phone. Keep in mind that this happened when the TV Jetsons were the only people who had cell phones. I left voice messages in both places telling him that we were stuck in the snow and asking him to please bring Todd home with him for lunch and that we would pick him up as quickly as possible. I traipsed back to the car that still hadn't moved from the snow-covered highway.

Feeling more hopeful because I had left the message explaining our delay, I calmed down a bit. Before too long, the cars started to move. We stopped at the closest gas station with a payphone and called again. This time, he answered. I was so relieved, but my relief quickly turned to panic again when I realized he didn't know what I was talking about. He hadn't gotten my message. He'd dropped Todd off at our house as usual. My car was parked in front of the house, and he'd assumed I was there. The front door was unlocked, so Todd just walked in and waved him off.

Have you ever prayed a panic prayer? No specifics, just pleas. My panic prayer was the same few words, repeated over and over during the ten-minute drive.

"Keep him safe. Keep him safe. Please, please, please keep him safe. Please, please, please keep him safe."

> My panic prayer was the same few words, "Keep him safe."

I was panicked that my three-and-a-half-year-old son was wandering the neighborhood streets in the snow, searching for us, wearing no coat or boots.

"Keep him safe."

I pictured him crying his little heart out in fear because he couldn't find anyone in the house.

"Keep him safe."

I was afraid he'd turned the stove on.

"Keep him safe."

We got home, and I ran into the house to find Todd sitting on the living room couch with our dog Nicki curled up next to him as he was watching a show on TV (probably Nickelodeon) and eating those tasteless little raw carrots. There was no fear in his face, no swollen eyes, no accidents in the house. Just a boy and his dog having a moment together. The dog had a bit of a guilty look, as I remember. That was understandable since she wasn't allowed on the couch. And she looked very surprised when I praised her and thanked her and told her she was the best! I was surprised too.

I asked Todd recently if he remembered that incident. He did. And he remembered the carrot detail, which I had forgotten. His recollection was of confusion but not panic. He wasn't nervous because Nicki was there, and she was excited to see him, so he took his cues from her. He remembers being comforted by having his dog right there with him in this unexpected grown-up situation.

God answered my prayer. He used the very thing I didn't really want in my home to comfort my precious child. There is a story in the Bible where Jesus and his disciples were in a boat in a storm, too, and they were just as panicked as I was. Jesus was right there on the boat, but he was sleeping. They woke him up, shouting. Jesus rebuked the wind and told the waves to be still. The disciples wondered why the winds and waves obeyed him. I experienced that kind of moment during the February snowstorm. Jesus calmed my storm. Not the actual snowstorm but the emotional storm within my heart. Even the winds and waves of worry obey him. And God used our black Lab puppy to answer my panic prayers that day.

BARB SYVERTSON enjoys writing about everyday experiences where God's love is obvious. Although she is retired from full-time library work, she still loves to stay busy. In addition to her writing, she spends time with her eight grandkids or on art, quilting, lunches with friends, board games, puzzles, and enjoying the Adirondack Mountains in New York. Her email address is barbsyvertson@gmail.com, and she welcomes your feedback.

"Tails" of Trust and Divine Lessons

JENNIFER ROSARIO

PLOPPED DOWN ON THE SOFA and swiped open my phone. In the notes section, I read from my prayer list, "God, give me the cutest, sweetest beagle." I looked up to heaven, grinned, and clicked open the website that matches you with dogs across the US. After a few minutes of searching, my grin faded, and my excitement waned. I had been checking for weeks.

Then, one miraculous day, the cutest beagle with a towel draped across his head came across my screen. "This is the one!" I said, immediately sending my request to the adoption agency. Before I knew it, I was on my way to South Carolina to pick up Luke, an adorable six-year-old beagle with hazelnut-colored eyes.

A few weeks in, and I thought God must have misheard me. While Luke was cute and sweet, he was quite raucous. He ate a cabinet in my brand-new house. He gobbled down a bag of popcorn, two dozen cookies, and a loaf of bread in his adjustment period. He was quite the handful. But after some time and patience, he began to trust me. His whole demeanor changed. Over the months, something in me changed too.

I started to see that the more Luke got to know me, the more trust he had in me. It occurred to me that this was the same kind of unrestrained trust I needed to have in God.

Trusting God's Provision

Luke loves to eat. I've never seen a dog get more excited about food than Luke. When I turn the knob to the pantry, he jumps and spins around like a tiny tornado. During this food dance, he's been known to knock over his water bowl and even me. I laugh and say, "Don't you know I'm going to feed you?"

I would never let Luke go hungry. I've spent money on him like someone would their child—biscuits and treat bowls, two different beds, shampoos, name tags. The list goes on and on. Luke doesn't spend one second worrying about these things. He goes through life knowing I will meet all his basic (and not-so-basic!) needs.

> Looking back, I've never gone hungry.

There have been many times in my life when I didn't have enough money or I didn't have a job. There have been times when I worried about what I was going to make for dinner, and there have been numerous complaints over the years regarding skyrocketing prices. But looking back, I've never gone hungry. I've always had exactly what I needed and, often, even more than what was needed. God has provided for me in the very same way I have for Luke. After all, I am his child, and his love for me is unmatched.

Trusting God's Protection

I often question Luke's peripheral vision. His snout can pick up the scent of a bone a mile away, but if I throw a treat to his right or left, he doesn't flinch. On walks, he doesn't always pay attention to where he is going, either. Because of this, he's stepped into holes, gotten his leash tangled in a wire, and even landed in a mud puddle. I try my best to watch out for him, but I don't always know what he's going to do next. Sometimes, I have to tug his leash gently and say, "Watch out." Luke is oblivious, but from my vantage point, I see the pitfalls and pests on the path that he doesn't always see.

There have been many times in my life when God has closed a door that I wanted to go through. At the time, I couldn't understand why, but this was God's gentle call to "watch out." God knows that I live with limited vision, but he can see the beginning from the end. And just as I carefully watch out for Luke and protect him from harmful objects on the path, I now see the same gentle tugs in my life as God protects me from the dangers only he can see.

Trusting God's Comfort

Like many dogs, Luke cannot stand loud noises. At the sound of thunder or fireworks, he jumps on top of me in search of solace. I try my best to make him feel safe. I hold him in my arms. I talk to him. I repeat again and again, "It's OK. It's only thunder." As much as I try to explain, there isn't much I can do. Luke doesn't understand. All he knows is that there are threatening sounds echoing all around him.

I finally found one thing that keeps him calm. We have to go into my dark closet and lie down on the floor. Yes, both of us! I lie on the floor with Luke to bring him some comfort. Eventually, his panting slows down, and he falls asleep.

> God sat there with me, offering peace.

In my life, I have felt tremendous fear more times than I can count. From airplanes to moving across the ocean, there have been many times when fear gripped me. God would try to comfort me with his Word, but like Luke, my heart raced, and I couldn't be stilled. In those times, God sat there with me, offering peace until I settled into his embrace.

IT TOOK A FEW MONTHS, but through my consistent care and love, Luke came to understand that I am someone he can trust. Trust is something that grows over time. I have walked with God for many years. It almost seems silly that I would doubt his love for me. Again and again, he has shown himself to be trustworthy. He is my faithful companion. Who or what shall I fear? I should take a cue from Luke, then, and rest in knowing that there is Someone looking after me and taking care of me every minute of every day.

JENNIFER ROSARIO is a Christian teacher, author, and screenwriter from Miami, Florida. She has a passion for writing and using her gifts to inspire and encourage others. Her songs and poems reflect the road from darkness into God's glorious light, while her various writing projects seek to encourage people with stories of hope and freedom. You can learn more at: www.jenniferrosarioauthor.com.

A Four-Legged Blessing

DIANA LEAGH MATTHEWS

A S I PUSHED OPEN THE front door to my rental home, quietness echoed throughout the rooms. "It would be so nice to have a dog." However, I knew this was not the time. Ten-plus-hour workdays filled my week. It wouldn't be fair to an animal to be home alone for half the day, every day.

So, I shoved the desire aside and threw myself into work, becoming a workaholic to the point of burnout.

Then within six months, my job ended due to a corporate takeover. I moved three hours away to help care for my ninety-seven-year-old grandmother, and I started a new job.

Occasionally, I would look at the humane society and other pet rescues, wishing and longing for a companion. It still wasn't the time for an animal. Caregiving and work took all my energy.

Fourteen months after I returned to my hometown, my grandmother passed away, and I had to adjust to another change.

An Answered Prayer

About a month had passed when I prayed, "Lord, I need someone to love and who will love me in return." I really had no idea who or what I was asking for.

After that prayer, I put the thought out of my mind until about two weeks later when a co-worker mentioned they were looking to rehome one of their dogs.

Two days later, I met Bentley, a Maltese Shih Tzu mix. The moment he was placed in my arms, I cradled his ten-pound body the way one would a baby. We stared at one another, and love filled my heart. It seemed we both knew that we'd found our forever person.

> We stared at one another, and love filled my heart.

My co-worker explained that Bentley and his siblings had been left on the side of the road at around a month old. Their family had fostered him for a year but had twelve children (half still at home) and four other dogs. The other dogs were carrying Bentley around in their mouths and bullying him, and the family decided he may be better off as an only child (or pooch).

Bentley nestled next to me on the drive home. It took him a few days to adjust, but within a short time, it seemed he'd always been with me.

Building Trust

My greatest scare came just six days after I got him when he bolted out the door and down the street. We're not far from several busy roads, and I prayed he didn't get too close to them as I chased after him.

At one point, he came near one of those busy roads, and I screamed, "Bentley, stop!" For the first time, he listened, and a few moments later, I caught him. In hindsight, I realized that was the moment he came to trust me.

Bentley has brought so much joy to my life, and he knows how to pull on my heartstrings. When I leave, he will nestle his head on my shoulder as if to say, "Do you have to go?" A few times, water filled his eyes, or tears fell down his cheeks. Talk about a gut punch. It made leaving for the workday or going to church even more difficult. However, he's rarely home alone. While I work, he spends the day with his Nonna.

When I arrive home, Bentley will run around me or lift onto his hind legs to be picked up, and then he kisses me to say, "I'm glad you're home." Then it's time for us to take a walk or play ball.

Bentley has forced me to be more active—which I needed— whether it's playing with his toys, practicing tricks, or going for a walk. Sometimes, we'll go to a local park or cemetery to walk instead of around the same old block. One of our favorites is slow dancing to "Puppy Love." He'll often stare into my eyes as I hold him and move to the music.

And he loves car rides. His ears will perk up at the mention, and he's eager to go. As long as he's with me, he seems happy. I buckle him into the back seat, and off we go. He waits patiently while I pump gas or we pull through one of his favorite drive-throughs. He will eagerly greet the window attendant and knows the ones who provide him with extra treats.

A Little Personality

Bentley can be a little particular, and it didn't take long for his personality to shine through. When we pick up a pup cup from the ice cream shop, I ask for his favorite: whipped cream. While he doesn't like vanilla ice cream (I guess it's too plain), he loves caramel or strawberry or peach ice cream.

Cold and creamy dishes aren't the only thing he's particular about. He refuses to eat dog food at all, preferring human food. I've talked with his vet to determine what he can and can't eat. He also refuses to dine on the same meal two times in a row. So, if there are leftovers, I have to be sure to alternate it with something else.

Then there's the matter of bowls. He doesn't like to put his face down into anything, so I purchased plates from the dollar store.

He prefers to drink from the trough of his to-go bottle rather than a bowl.

All these peculiarities lead to laughter and fond remembrances of my grandmother. It's amazing how similar their characteristics are at times. Bentley has stairs to our bay window and loves to watch all the comings and goings on the street. Besides, there are the birds and passersby to watch as well.

Then there are the side glances he gives me, the same way my grandmother did. And although he never met my grandmother, he's taken with her chair.

Plus, they both love presents. When he was the only one not to receive a present for Mother's Day, he gave me a look that said, "Where's mine?" and his eyes watered. My heart broke.

Oh, and when I told him he's a dog, well, I received the silent treatment for several hours. So, we refer to him as a pooch instead.

The Joy of His Antics

Bentley has brought so much laughter, as well.

Mama had two major surgeries within ten months of one another, so we moved in to care for her. After her neck surgery, she could not move her head for over three months. We placed a full-length mirror in the hallway so she could make sure that Bentley wasn't underfoot.

At first, he didn't know what to think about the mirror. He would run up to it and stare at himself. Then he'd rear up on his hind legs and growl, but he looked more like a white stallion. When it seemed as if no one was watching, he'd prance in front of the mirror. Checking one side, making sure his tail was up, and adjusting his hips. Then he'd turn around to repeat with the other side. How could we not laugh? He was so adorable.

Bentley has a tender heart. While Nonna recovered from her surgeries, he'd lay beside her, providing comfort. They developed their own nap rituals. But even a sneeze or cough will send him running to make sure we're OK.

Bentley loves to be spoiled, and when we go to school, he races to speak to Ms. Deb, his trainer. The moment he sees her, he rolls over onto his back for a belly rub. He's come a long way from our first session, where he wouldn't even let Ms. Deb near him. Now, he can't wait to see her and obediently sits, waiting for his next command.

> All his schooling has prepared him for pet therapy certification.

All his schooling has prepared him for pet therapy certification. Bentley loves to go to "work" with Mommy. For him, this means going to several nursing homes to visit with the residents. He doesn't like others to hold him but loves to be petted and given treats. At times, he'll even show his friends a few of his tricks. Sometimes, he'll spin and twirl. Other times, he'll bow, and on occasion, he'll shake or give a high-five.

The residents are eager to see Bentley in his special outfit of the day on his visits. Mommy tells people, "He has a better wardrobe than I do." And that's true. All types of muscle shirts and T-shirts with cute sayings for the summer and sweaters and PJs for the winter. He even has his own kilt.

Recently, we attended an outdoor concert where he wore his overalls. While there, another Shih Tzu approached with her owner. Bentley wasn't sure about Daisy and wouldn't let the other pooch step too close. However, Daisy stared at him throughout the entire concert and surely would have loved to have been friends.

The Child I Always Wanted

Bentley seems to only have eyes for his mommy, though. He loves his snugs, and when there are thunderstorms, Mommy will put his robe on him and rock him in her arms.

In many ways, Bentley has become the child I never had and always wanted. Often, I'll hold him in one arm while carrying out household chores such as emptying the dishwasher, starting a load of laundry, or picking up. I have a bookshelf full of children's books, and each night, we'll read a story. He'll lay his head back against my chest to listen.

One of the last things we do before bed is say nighttime prayers. Bentley bends his front paws to make "prayer paws." He treats it like a sacred time and closes his eyes and sometimes even lays his head against my chest. Afterward, he is so cute because he makes the rounds to ensure the house is ready for bedtime.

He's brought me so much joy and happiness, and I can't imagine not having Bentley in my life. Whether he's pressed against me as I write, eagerly greeting me when I arrive home, or staring at me to say, "It's time to play," he's always happy to have me nearby.

I'm delighted to have him. He's given my life meaning and purpose, eased the loneliness, lifted the depression, and provided more love than I deserve. Each day together is a blessing, and I can't help but say, "Thank you, Lord, for Bentley." Hopefully, many more years are ahead for us.

The Lord knew the perfect timing when he answered my prayer. He provided me with someone to love, and he sent someone who loved me, as well.

DIANA LEAGH MATTHEWS shares God's love through her story from rebel to redeemed. She provides programs as a speaker, teacher, and life coach and presents historical monologues. Leagh's (pronounced Lee) debut novel *Carol of the Rooms* was a Realm Award finalist. Her second novel, *Forever Changed*, releases in winter 2025. Visit her at DianaLeaghMatthews.com to learn more and sign up for her monthly newsletter.

Just What the Doctor Ordered

ROBIN GRUNDER

IT'S FUNNY HOW I SIT here with my very own therapy dog—petting her, loving her, speaking to her in a baby-talk voice—and how this seems to help me in my current situation. It's not laugh-out-loud funny, but funny in a full-circle way of looking at a situation that can only be seen in hindsight.

When Ripley (aka Rip, aka Biggie, aka my precious big girl, aka *Ripley's Believe It or Not*) first came to live with us, she was all puppy. All *big* puppy. We could tell by her paws that she would be a big dog, which is not uncommon with Bernese Mountain Dogs. It was important to me to have a well-trained big dog since she would be spending time with our grandkids. Our Wednesday evenings were spent training with other dogs and handlers.

Ripley loved school. You know how some dog parents have to spell out the word *walk*, or their dog will go bonkers waiting to go on that walk? Ripley was the same way about the word *school*.

"Ripley, are you ready to go to school?" She was out the door and waiting by the car before the question was asked. The same was true if I asked her if she wanted to see her *friends*.

Rip thrived in her training. She was eager to please and very social and well-behaved around the other dogs and handlers. It made her so happy to "go to school" and be around others—two and four-legged. It wasn't hard to take her through the Canine Good Citizen test so she could be a certified therapy dog. I call her my "certified good girl."

Right around Ripley's six-month-old mark, I noticed she was looking a bit clumsy. She was seventy pounds, so she was not full size for a Berner. She still did so well with training and loved going on therapy visits to schools, libraries, and kids' clubs. She loved being groomed and even hugged me with two paws wrapped around my neck at every chance she could get. Her clumsiness did not seem to be associated with any outward signs of pain. I chalked it up to being a big puppy who had not gotten used to her size.

> She hugged me with two paws wrapped around my neck at every chance she could get.

But then her clunky vibe started looking more like a struggle than normal puppy growing pains, even needing help getting up from a seated or down position. X-rays revealed that our big-hearted Berner had severe hip dysplasia. After consulting with two veterinarians, the breeder we got her from, and an orthopedic specialist, her prognosis did not look promising. She would need a total hip replacement for her to live a full, long life.

We had to wait a few more months until Ripley was done growing to know if she was a good candidate for a hip replacement. During our wait, she continued to go to her "school" once a month and went on more therapy dog visits, mostly letting children read to her at libraries and visiting college campuses during finals week. Ripley's superpower was bringing smiles to faces that had not smiled for a while. And I cannot tell you how often a parent has come up to me to say that their child struggles to read, but he or she will read out loud to Rip. Dogs don't judge when you read to them. They look in your eye and love you while you do. That's another of her superpowers.

She was a regular at Eastern Iowa Community College. On one visit, we arrived a little early to visit the library staff, who knew Ripley by name. When we arrived, a student ID with Ripley's name and photo was waiting for us. They made Rip an honorary student, and she paid her tuition in big pet pets, hugs, slobbery kisses, and lots and lots of fur.

> They made Rip an honorary student, and she paid her tuition in big pet pets, hugs, slobbery kisses, and lots and lots of fur.

As Rip approached her first birthday, we had some new X-rays done to show the bone growth and to see if she was ready for a brand-new hip. The new images showed that Rip's case was unique and severe in how both hips rolled up above the barely formed hip sockets. The surgeon was able to consult with one of the top specialists in the county, who gave us some more insight.

The first insight was that both of her hips needed to be replaced. The second was that Ripley was at an increased risk of needing additional surgeries due to how the joints in her legs adapted to the hips not being properly formed. There were no guarantees that our Biggie Berner Girl would get any better, even with surgical intervention.

After all the consulting and a lot of crying, we decided not to move forward with the double hip replacement and continue with medical management. She takes two medicines and one supplement daily and continues to look and act like a big puppy. We were told she could live this way for a few months or a few years—there were no guarantees. We've learned to take it one day at a time.

I continued to take her on her therapy visits, which she loved every bit as much as the people she would go see. She became a regular at a local bank where everyone from every office in that building knew her by name. At libraries, kids couldn't wait to show Ripley the book they wanted to read to her. She brought joy, comfort, smiles, and confidence to everyone she interacted with.

IT'S BEEN TWO YEARS SINCE Rip's diagnosis. She is doing far better than the doctors predicted, but unfortunately, I cannot take Rip on therapy visits anymore. She just got to be too big for me to help her in and out of my car. And as it turned out, the two of us have more in common than I could have predicted.

> The two of us have more in common than I could have predicted.

Last year, I was diagnosed with chronic, severe osteoarthritis. My most urgent symptom was pain that radiated from my neck to the left side of my face. Images showed that arthritis in my neck was pinching a specific nerve between my top two vertebrae. The fix was surgical. Since then, I've had multiple joints flare up with no fixes except joint replacement or fusion. And just like a page from Ripley's life, I can't go up and down stairs or move well without assistance. It's as if I've aged thirty years over the last two, and my bones don't seem to care about how that math does not add up.

My prognosis and treatment options for pain relief are also not promising. For the last two years, my life has revolved around physical therapy, cortisone injections, and more surgeries. The physical side of it also makes itself known mentally. It's all a struggle, made a little more manageable with a very special, very specific type of therapy—Ripley.

At three years old, Rip isn't attending school or therapy visits with others. But as I sit here petting and talking to her, I know it is just as good, if not better, than anything either of our doctors have ordered.

When other people look at our Ripley, they might see a big dog with an off-balance gait. But all I see is her big heart and her ability to bring a smile to my face when nothing else seems to work.

It's still her superpower.

Robin Grunder is a journalist, author, ghostwriter, and executive editor of Legacy Press Books. Her work has been featured in *Chicken Soup for the Soul,* regional and national parenting publications, newspapers, and several ghostwritten books. She is the author of *Memoir in the Margins of Psalms: Journaling Your Life-Story in the Margins of God's Story.* Robin and her husband, Brian, have a blended family of seven adult children and three grandchildren. Visit Robin at www.robingrunder.org.

Akers, the Seeing Eye Eagle

LISA J. RADCLIFF

MY FAMILY EAGERLY AWAITED THE arrival of our sixteenth Seeing Eye® puppy. It wasn't supposed to be Akers. The Seeing Eye had assigned us another dog, but then Akers was born and named after Philadelphia Eagles kicker David Akers. Since I was a staff member in the puppy development department of The Seeing Eye, Inc. and a huge Eagles fan, my original assignment was changed. Akers was given to my family to raise, while Bartram (named for the Eagles long-snapper) was raised by the only other Eagles fan on staff. Eagles fans in North Jersey are few and far between.

I knew the moment I saw him Akers was going to be a handful. He arrived in my office outfitted in a New York Giants jersey, and the fur on his snout formed a mohawk. He was an adorable, fluffy, amber-colored Lab/Golden Retriever cross. The look in his eyes said he was ready to play. He was going to live up to his namesake's reputation for mischief.

Akers was a fun puppy. I was sure he did things just to make us laugh. His one negative—he had a habit of chewing holes in our hardwood floors. He hid it well. I would hear him chewing something and take a look. Akers would look up at me innocently, with a toy between his front paws. His expression seemed to convey, "What? I'm not doing anything naughty."

This exchange happened several times. He really looked innocent, and I felt bad for assuming he was doing something wrong. But when he got up to move from that spot, there was a hole in the floor. It was hard to stay mad at him with that sweet, mohawked face.

> It was hard to stay mad at him with that sweet, mohawked face.

Akers's love for chewing or eating things that weren't edible didn't stop at wooden floors. Seeing Eye puppies sleep on a short bed tie-down so that they are used to it when they go home with their blind person. The person must know exactly where the dog is if they need them, even during the night. Somehow, Akers managed to get onto our son's bed and pull his glasses from the headboard—while hooked to an eighteen-inch tie-down. When I woke my son the next morning, his glasses were unrecognizable, just a mangle of metal and no glass (we found the lenses later). They were only a week old, so I took them back and held them out to the eyeglass store employee, saying, "They broke."

She responded, "They sure did." They replaced them, and my son was much more careful from then on.

The pup was my sidekick for the favorite part of my job: talking about The Seeing Eye with all sorts of groups, from the smallest Girl Scouts to large corporations. Akers's favorite was the school groups because the kids made such a fuss over him. Toward the end of his training, we did a talk at an elementary school. The teacher told me just before we started our presentation that the kids weren't allowed to touch the dogs. I wondered how Akers would feel about that. We stood at the door as the kids filed out, waving to Akers but not touching him. He kept looking at me as if something was very wrong. He sulked about it all the way home. I tried to explain to him that some schools have rules. He wasn't buying it. He was offended.

> He sulked about it all the way home. I tried to explain to him that some schools have rules.

Akers grew into a beautiful, confident dog. On a trip to Washington, DC, we realized that Akers was a city dog. It was very crowded, but Akers was more relaxed there than ever before. We had high expectations for him as he returned to The Seeing Eye for formal training. I had no doubt that he would make a great Seeing Eye dog. Sure enough, Akers flew through his formal training and was placed with a woman in New York City.

"No! Not New York. Not a Giants fan." Maybe she was a Jets fan. Akers could adjust to that.

I spoke with his instructor a few times during training and after he was placed. He went out to check Akers's work because the woman had a few concerns. He didn't seem to know which house was theirs. They lived in a row home in Brooklyn. I suppose it would be hard for anyone to tell one home from another if you can't read the numbers. So, the instructor went out to check on Akers.

As Akers came down the street and close to their home, he got excited, wagging his tail in anticipation. He glanced up at his owner a few times, then turned up a walkway a few houses from their own. Once his master realized it was the wrong house, she corrected him, and with a bounce in his step, he led her down the walk and directly to their home. The instructor's assessment of the situation was that Akers knew exactly what he was doing. He was playing a joke on her. He knew which house it was, but at the end of a day guiding his master through the challenges of New York City, why not have a little fun?

Unfortunately, after only three years, Akers's owner became ill and was unable to work him. Having no one to care for him, she returned Akers to The Seeing Eye. He was just past the age to be retrained for someone else. They called us and asked if we would take him back as a pet. He was five years old and taking early retirement. We were thrilled about the opportunity to have him as part of our family.

It took him about eight months to stop running to the door every time one of us went near it or touched a leash. He was still ready and willing to work. But one of his new joys was swimming. He wasn't allowed in the pool as a puppy, but now that he was retired, Akers loved to jump in with the rest of us. He fancied himself a lifeguard. I'm not sure what my swimming stroke looked like, but to Akers, it looked like I needed rescuing. Every time I was swimming, Akers jumped in to save me.

He learned to use the ladder to exit so as not to scratch the pool liner. Even better than the pool was the lake where we vacationed in Maine. He loved swimming, but more, he loved jumping into the water. In Maine, he could jump in from the dock, the beach, and the rocks that offered him natural diving boards of all heights. He didn't just jump; he launched himself high in the air and hit the water in a seismic splash.

> Akers was a perfect big brother and mentor to the many Seeing Eye puppies who came after him.

Akers was a perfect big brother and mentor to the many Seeing Eye puppies who came after him. He seemed to enjoy his new role as a mentor. Although, sometimes he looked at a puppy doing something it shouldn't and back at me as if he was saying, "This one doesn't have a chance." And he was so gentle and easy to handle that our three-year-old granddaughter could walk him.

> He was so gentle and easy to handle that our three-year-old granddaughter could walk him.

When my father-in-law moved into our home on hospice, Akers was his constant companion. I was fearful that he was more of a speed bump and worried that Dad would trip over him. But Akers was always careful to move out of the way. The last two days before Dad passed, Akers refused to leave his room, even at bedtime. He seemed to know the end was near, and he wouldn't leave Dad to face it alone.

A year later, Akers faced his own health crisis. At eleven years old, he was behaving strangely, not himself. He would sometimes sit in the corner of the family room, facing the wall, panting heavily. It was strange. Then there were times he wouldn't go outside. He would lie on the floor, watching everyone but not moving. I called the vet. They took an X-ray, thinking maybe he had swallowed something that got stuck.

Some things hadn't changed, except he chose to eat mostly edible things, like a box of crackers. But he would eat the crackers and the box. We had to Akers-proof our kitchen cabinets. I imagined his blind person looking for groceries she was sure she bought, not knowing that Akers ate the food and left no evidence. When the vet returned from looking at the X-ray, she didn't say a word, just hugged me. "Cancer." "A few weeks." "I'm so sorry. He's such a sweet boy." We hugged again, both of us sobbing.

On his last day, he was stuck to me like glue. I had to leave him for an hour. When I returned home, Akers was lying in the hallway. I was there in time to see him take his last breath. I wept over him, telling him what a great dog he was, thanking him for his love and service. Stroking the mohawk that had turned from dark gold to white over the years, I said goodbye to the best dog I have known.

LISA J. RADCLIFF is an author and speaker in southeastern Pennsylvania. Lisa has been a homeschool mom, a puppy development coordinator at The Seeing Eye, Inc., and now writes and speaks full-time. Her most recent book, *A Time To Laugh: My Life Over Fifty*, highlights the joys of this season of life, especially the funny things grandchildren say. To reach Lisa, visit her website at www.lisajradcliff.com.

Playful Antics
and Adventure

The Punny Thing about Cats

MICHELLE RAYBURN

Cat-titude is everything,
I purr-sonally say.
Fur real, a cat has got to be
Most mewdy when they play.

I'll whisker a secret.
You have to be kitten.
It's paws-itively purr-fect,
I'm paws-sibly smitten.

They're catnip fanatics,
Cat's out of the bag.
This tail about felines
Is purr-haps a red flag.

The cat-astrophic cuteness
Is claws for celebration.
They're purr-plexingly coy,
Litter-al vexation.

The meow-gical moments
Purr-suade me to cheer.
Feline sappy about cats
Is mew-sic to their ears.

The tail-end of the poem,
The meow-ment has come.
Please whisker me luck
In the purr-suit of fun.

Time for cat-ching some Z's
Or some meow-velous sun.
Take a little cat nap
'Cause I'm meow out of puns.

MICHELLE RAYBURN is the publisher and managing editor of this book.

Pet Parties for Patches

MEL TAVARES

USK WAS UPON ME AS I hurried from the grocery store, intent on getting home and making dinner. Just two steps outside of the door, I encountered a young boy who began pleading with me. "Please, lady. Please take this little kitten. Nobody wants it because he's too scrawny, but my mama said I can't come home for dinner until there are no more kittens." I felt a twinge on my heartstrings.

I fought tears as I thought back to the painful goodbye I'd said to my fourteen-year-old German Shorthair dog not long before. While some families choose to add a new pet to the household immediately, we had not and were not sure we ever would again. Shannon had been such a wonderful pet and so much a part of our everyday lives that I just couldn't imagine being able to love another like I loved her. I'd grown up with many cats and dogs and had continued acquiring them as an adult. But Shannon was different, somehow feeling more human than dog.

"Please, lady, because I'm very hungry. Just take it so I can go home and eat dinner." His pleading interrupted my thoughts. One look at the tears sliding down the tender cheeks and my hurting heart softened. I reached out my hand and slipped the tiny kitten into the oversized pocket of my fall jacket. A smile lit up his face as he ran toward home, looking back only to wave and shout out one last thank you.

> Squeals of delight filled the room as my two young girls watched me carefully remove her from my pocket.

I drove home, stroking the soft fur of the runt of the litter, talking to her as she purred in response. Squeals of delight filled the room as my two young girls watched me carefully remove her from my pocket. "Look at the gray and white patches!" the oldest said. "Let's call her Patches!"

"She's hungry! Mommy, where's the food for her?"

Not wanting the girls to realize that I had forgotten the kitten would need food, or anything else for that matter, I turned away for just a moment. Trying not to panic, I turned back toward their eager faces and said, "Patches is a special kitty and deserves only the best! This can of tuna will feed her for days because she can only eat a little at a time!"

More squeals of delight pierced the air as I opened the can. "But Mommy, where is her dish?" *Oops.* Quickly reaching into the china cabinet, I pulled out a pedestal dessert dish. "Only the best for little Patches," I announced.

The girls shrieked with joy and said, "Patches, you are the queen, and we will treat you like the queen you are!"

Thankfully, people in our neighborhood also had cats. I called a friend and asked to borrow some kitty litter until I could get to the store the next day. While I created a temporary litter box using a cardboard tray, the girls watched Patches nibble tuna from the crystal dish.

Becoming Family

From that point forward, Patches enjoyed the best clothes, bed, and pampering. Two more kids were born during her lifespan, and the four siblings treated her as the fifth sibling. They dressed her up, pushed her around in a doll carriage, and argued about who got to have her in bed with them each night. Being the smallest of the litter, she didn't weigh much, even as an adult, and never lost the personality of her youth. I am thankful I heeded the pleadings of the little boy at the store and brought Patches home so the kids could enjoy having a pet.

When the kids asked if God likes people to have pets, I said the Bible doesn't explicitly talk about pets, but we do know that God created animals and wants us to care for them well. I told the kids that it is clear God not only created but also loves animals.

Pets Like Parties Too

We are a family that loves to celebrate often, and it always involves food and decorations. I was one of the pioneers of the pet party movement, always a firm believer in celebrating pets as much as we would any other family member. For sixteen years, we hosted parties for our beloved cat, Patches. As a member of the family, Patches also received gifts throughout the year and even had her own stocking hung at Christmas.

> I was one of the pioneers of the pet party movement.

No occasion is celebrated as much as a birthday, a day set aside for just one to be honored and recognized. Therefore, each year, on the second weekend of October, we created a birthday party just for Patches.

I'm old enough to have needed to create the pet parties for Patches without the help of Pinterest. Today, a quick search of the site will reveal lots of ideas for creating a pet party for furry friends. There are a few essential elements our family incorporates to make the party memorable.

Decorations are a must and can be as simple as pictures through the years hung on twine with clothes pins or as extravagant as balloons that spell the name of the furry family member. Games have included pin the tail on the cat and k-i-t-t-y (remixed bingo), which are easily tailored to feature dogs if needed. Activities to keep younger kids engaged included reading adventure stories featuring animals and making bookmarks.

As stated earlier, food is always central to our party themes, and over the years, I've made everything from "meow mix" (giving a different name to our favorite family snack mix recipe) to cat-shaped sandwiches or a full charcuterie-style Goldfish bar featuring all the different flavors of crackers.

> Just once a year, Patches was allowed to sit at the table.

The table was always set, and just once a year, Patches was allowed to sit at the table. The centerpiece of the party was her birthday cake, made of tuna, as you might have already guessed. The tuna cake commemorated the day we adopted her into the family , when she ate tuna because we had no cat food in the house. Dry cat food used to decorate her cake commemorated her eventual graduation to dry cat food.

Tearful Goodbyes

For sixteen years, all of us donned birthday party hats and let her sit at the table to eat her tuna cake while we sang Happy Birthday to her. But the time came to say goodbye just before her seventeenth birthday. We came home from an overnight camping trip and found her lying behind the washing machine, panting and lethargic. A visit to the vet revealed a stomach tumor that had gone undetected.

Just as it is hard to say goodbye to a human member of our family, so it is when giving a last hug to a furry member of our family. Thankfully, no one spoke platitudes to us, such as, "She lived a nice, long life."

> Tears flowed for days, and the house seemed empty.

Tears flowed for days, and the house seemed empty without her. October came, and there was a void in the calendar on the day that would have been filled with planning and preparation and tuna cake decorating. That year was somber as we struggled to figure out what to do with our time instead. We decided to tell stories about her and cherish the memories of how she transformed our lives as a precious part of the family.

Years later, siblings have moved to their own homes, and some carry on the pet party tradition for their furry family members. Although Patches is no longer with us, calls and texts are sent among the kids and me on her birthday as we fondly stroll down memory lane and recall all the parties we hosted for Patches.

MEL TAVARES has been adopting and writing about her family dogs and cats since elementary school. A story written about her tomcat was highly regarded by her English teacher and perpetuated his recommendation she become a writer. Today, Mel is a multi-published, award-winning writer and storyteller, as well as a best-selling book author. The Pinterest "Pet Parties" board link is Pinterest.com/DrMelTavares/pet-parties. Additional resources can be located on her website drmeltavares.com.

Sassy

PAULA HEMINGWAY

A MOVE TO A NEW NEIGHBORHOOD can be quite stressful, especially with six kids. This one from Texas to Arkansas was our sixteenth in our twenty-year marriage. As I unpacked the mountainous boxes that stood like pillars in every room of our new home, uncertainties clouded my thoughts. *Would the neighbors like us? Would we like them? What would they think of our large, sometimes loud, family?* To my dismay, I soon discovered one family's opinion of us wasn't flattering.

In the evenings, the elderly couple next door walked their frau-frau dog along the sidewalk in front of our house and cast disapproving glances our way as if we'd done something wrong. I figured they must not love kids, worried they might ruin property values. One day as I backed our huge van loaded with children out of the driveway, Mrs. Grump, with her disdainful looks, suddenly appeared as she strolled along with her lovely and perfect pet. When she approached our driveway, I braked to allow her to cross. She must have had the same thought and stopped for me. As soon as I decided to go ahead, she also decided to go ahead.

I finally waved her on. She looked at me in disgust and muttered some choice words under her breath.

Irritated with her grouchy attitude, I felt a strong urge to roll down the car window and shout something like, "You're mean. And ugly!" But I thought better of it, being a Christian and all. It might ruin my witness. Even though I didn't want to, I determined to treat her as Jesus would, with kindness and respect. I rolled the car window down, smiled sweetly, and said, "You sure have a pretty dog." She grunted a response as she continued down the sidewalk. *This woman really does not like me.* That was a problem.

As we settled into our new home and met other neighbors, Mr. and Mrs. Grump remained as snooty as their pup. We couldn't figure out why the Grumps didn't like us. We're friendly, our six cherubs divine (well, mostly), and we kept our lawn mowed. What's not to like? Maybe they didn't like Texans who owned a low-class mutt that should never be seen in the same yard with their elegant Miss Highbrow.

> Mr. and Mrs. Grump remained as snooty as their pup.

Yes, we were baffled but decided to take on the challenge to get them to smile at least once.

I laughed the day my husband, Mark, burst into the house from his yard work, whooping as if he'd won a prize. He shouted, "I found out the dog's name! Her name is Sassy!" What a perfect name for a pampered pooch with persnickety parents.

Now we could put "Operation Bow-Wow" into action. Every time we saw the canine cutie strut by with her humanoid on the other end of the leash, we called out, "Hi, Sassy!" Mrs. Sassy almost split her lips into a smile but quickly muzzled any friendliness that might bubble up. The only tail wagging from this duo effervesced from the classy critter with the rhinestone collar. What was it going to take to arrive at the pleasant state of congeniality with these people? We didn't have to be best friends. Common courtesy would be good, but apparently, that wasn't in their repertoire. We were stumped. Maybe we should give up.

> We were stumped. Maybe we should give up.

Nevertheless, despite our lack of success, we remained undaunted and resolved to take our game plan to the next level.

The next step in making friends with Sassy's humans was to carry on a conversation with the four-legged tyke. "Hi, Sassy, how are you?" or "You sure look cute today." Gradually, over a longer period than anyone would think possible, Mr. and Mrs. Rottweiler softened into Mr. and Mrs. Tolerable. This small triumph wasn't enough to form a friendship between us, and their presence continued to make me nervous as a poodle at the groomer's. Even though our pooch plan pranced forward, it seemed we needed divine intervention to cancel my vote for them as "Worst Neighbors of the Year." Little did I realize that God *was* about to intervene and fast forward the action.

Another neighbor, a "nice" one, shared that Sassy's dad had recently been in the hospital for surgery, and although he would recover, he had a serious condition. That evening, while fixing supper for my family, I thought about my neighbors and my favorite Teacher of long ago who said, "If you love only those who love you, what reward is there for that? Even corrupt tax collectors do that much" (Matthew 5:46). As I prayed for them, I felt God tell me, not in an audible voice but nonetheless clearly, to fix a meal for this caustic couple.

Wait a minute. Praying for them was one thing, but serving them was quite another. I reminded God that these people didn't like me or my family, lacked kindness, and frankly, I was afraid of their rejection. Furthermore, I was simply dog-tired of trying to get them to like us. I didn't like God's food service plan, and I didn't like "them." So there!

After two days of struggle back and forth with God, I knew I had to trust him to help me minister to my unpleasant neighbors. As I prepared what I hoped would be a delicious and comforting meal for them, my heart pounded. It also changed. My desire switched from gaining their approval to serving them in the same way I would serve Jesus and people I love.

> I trudged over to Sassy's house with my delicious meal and five-year-old daughter in tow.

With fear in my heart, I trudged over to Sassy's house with my delicious meal and five-year-old daughter in tow. I figured when they saw Laura's cuteness, they might loosen up, which would increase my chances of a good outcome. Many thoughts swirled in my brain. *What if they yell at me? What if they don't like lasagna? What if my food makes them sick? Then they'll really hate me.* When I arrived at their porch, my heart beat faster as I stared at the door. *Don't chicken out now.* I forced my hand to knock, secretly hoping they wouldn't be home so I could get out of the situation and then could tell God I had tried.

Surprise! Mrs. Tolerable opened the door. I smiled and said, "Hi. I'm your neighbor, Paula. I heard about your husband's health situation and am so sorry. We have been praying for him. How is he doing?"

She replied pleasantly, as if we were old friends, "He's doing well." After a short chat, she took the meal and thanked me.

I almost skipped back home as I thanked God for the miracle of our neighbors' softened hearts and my own changed heart that now contained much hope for future friendliness between our two families.

This experience taught me to act when God calls despite my fear. When I answer yes to God's call, many blessings come. When I answer no, I miss the blessings. God's plan is always better than mine. Sure, my worst fear could have happened with a slam of the neighbors' door. That act of rejection would have brought sadness and distress, but I would find comfort in my obedience to God.

God not only broke down the relationship barrier with our neighbors, but he also forged a friendship between us. Our new friends invited Laura over to play with Sassy several times. They shared interesting stories with us about the previous owners of our home. When he recuperated, Sassy's dad came to our house a few times to help me with some of my projects.

Although we never became best friends, we lived in harmony. Now, when Mr. and Mrs. Friendly walked by with Sassy, we waved, and they often stopped to talk.

What a miraculous transformation through a sassy little dog and God's divine intervention!

Paula Hemingway, married to Mark Hemingway for forty-nine years, mother of six children, and Grammie to twenty-two grandchildren, loves to play the piano, tennis, pickleball, and cornhole. Sometimes she plays at writing, but her favorite play is with her grandkids. Paula's stories of family life have been published in three Guideposts books, *Mature Living Magazine*, *The Secret Place*, *Laundry Tales to Lighten Your Load*, and *The One Year Devotional of Joy and Laughter.*

A Dog's Christmas

MARCIA OKERLUND

It was days before Christmas and down on North Gale,
the dogs were uneasy, each one with a tale.
The stockings were hung by Connie and Jim,
in hopes that they soon would be filled to the brim.

Each dog was tucked in, with blanket on bed,
quiet and lonely, thoughts of a home running through
    each head.
Arthur in collar, and Molly in bow,
were feeling quite sad; their spirits seemed low.
Sammi noticed their downcast and quickly replied,
"Why do you fret when you're cozy and warm and inside?"

"But," added Ricky, "can you not see?
No one wants you, and certainly not me!
Do you really think anyone cares if we die or we live?
There are hundreds of us and no thought do they give!"

"Where, oh, where did you get such a notion?
The volunteers help us with so much devotion!"

Just then from the outside there arose such a clatter,
the dogs all wondered, *What is the matter?*
Looking out of the window, they couldn't believe;
was it for real, or did their dark eyes deceive?

Then, Sammi re-*bark*ed, "Look, a group of old friends
    is here.
They each give their time year after year.

"Mark with a hammer and Mike with a plow
are ready for snow, whether later or now.
Jann, equipped with a camera in hand,
will snap all our pictures and make us look grand.
Dave and John are all set to mow, keeping the grass short
    and ready for fun,
So, when it is time, we can get out and run.

"Leanne, Lynn, and Cheryl, with fosters in tow,
train the puppy mill dogs so to nice homes they can go.
Pregnant ladies come in wondering, *What will I do?*
Oh, where will they go? There's more than a few.
But Bobbi opens her arms exceptionally wide,
willing to take one to twenty, all in her stride.

"Dawn teaches the new volunteers the tricks of the trade
while Janie makes phone calls to ensure we are spayed.
Our wonderful friends drop off empty cans, whether
    soda or beer,
so, Tracy can deliver to the refund cashier.
Mo writes out cards—so many to thank,
while Annie prepares the deposits, ready to bank.

"There stands Gordy, Lisa, Bruce, Karen, Michael and Joe,
With leash in hand and boots for the snow.
Charlie and Patty are ready to scoop,
For in the yard there is sure to be poop.

"Each year is a yard sale; there's so much to do.
Every volunteer team forms quite a large crew.
Friends on the outside bring items galore.
When we think they are done, they collect even more.
For two days we draw a large crowd of shoppers seeking
    to find,
those items that might be one of a kind.

"Maryann thanks the sponsors who help pay the bills,
for heating, electric, and sometimes our pills.
Toni is here as one of the elves,
with arms full of goodies to load up the shelves.

"Many drive in at all times of the day,
making time in their schedules, getting away
to bring sheets, blankets, bedding, and such.
All of these things we appreciate much.

"We have other companions that live far away,
they, too, have no home and no place to stay.
So, wonderful drivers like Linda and Steve
drive mile after mile for them to retrieve.

"Gwen sits and ponders to write all the grants,
to help meet every need, even some in advance.
The isolation room, or maybe a roof,
to make sure that our home is now weatherproof.
Four thousand dogs have passed through this door,
And with continued support, there'll be four thousand
    more.

"So, you see, little Ricky, what volunteers give,
to make sure that you're comfy in the place that you live."

"I do see! I know that I'm loved and cared for right now.
We need to do something for them; I just don't know
    how!"

"Well, it's now that wonderful time of the year,
That gives us a chance to send season's cheer.
To sponsors, adopters, businesses, friends far and near,
We say, 'Thank you, Merry Christmas, and Happy
    New Year!'"

MARCIA OKERLUND grew up on a farm in western New York with her best friends, Jinx, Snooks, Phillippe, and her horse, Moonshine. Always one to rescue the stray or injured, Marcia has nursed baby birds, an opossum, and a squirrel named Bonkers. She's been a volunteer at the Northern Chautauqua Canine Rescue for over twenty years and served eleven years as the director.

Dog Days of Summer

PAM WHITLEY TAYLOR

ONLY SECONDS BEFORE OUR SON, Ben, walked in the door from school, we closed the flaps of the cardboard box to hide his rambunctious one-of-a-kind birthday gift. Ben had wanted a puppy for several years, and his dad and I had always said, "Not now."

But as I lamented to a friend that we had no idea what to get Ben for his fifteenth birthday, she had a suggestion. A friend of hers was selling Schnauzer puppies that would be weaned in six weeks. That meant they'd be available by Ben's April birthday.

She'd seen them and said that the smallest one of the litter was adorable. "I think Ben and Jan need him."

Through the years, I'd balked on the idea of a pet because of two concerns. Our daughter, Jan, was multiple-handicapped, and I wasn't sure how a pet would relate to her. And my number two concern, I must admit, was selfish. I didn't want one more responsibility, and I thought a pet would probably turn out to be mine to take care of.

Even though I still had my doubts, as my hubby and I talked it over, we decided if we were ever going to get Ben a dog, it was now or never. Ultimately, we made up our minds that we'd surprise him with his long overdue wish.

My husband took off work on the morning of Ben's birthday, which was also the pick-up-the-pup day. We rushed around, getting ready for our new charge. We bought Puppy Chow, bowls for food and water, a dog leash, doggie pads, and everything else we thought a puppy might need.

Then a few hours before Ben was due home, we drove to the lady's house to meet our little fella for the first time. He was as adorable as my friend had said, and I fell in love with him at first glance. We were all the more excited about Ben's gift and couldn't wait for Ben to meet him.

On that April day when Ben walked in the front door, we hollered, "Surprise!"

> He saw the big box with a bow and could tell it was moving.

He saw the big box with a bow and could tell it was moving and had sound effects. With a quizzical look, he eagerly walked over and pulled open the flaps to see what was inside. He scooped the puppy into his arms, beaming with excitement. I think I saw a few tears in his eyes as he asked, "Is this for real? Is he mine?"

I think he was a bit shocked, but he recovered quickly and named his puppy Jake. Jake quickly became a cherished member of our family. And to my great surprise, Jake seemed to have a sixth sense about Jan.

Jan was much like a two-to-six-month-old but in an eleven-year-old-sized body that didn't work. She was also non-verbal. To our great surprise, that sweet puppy seemed to understand that she had special needs. Shockingly, even as a puppy, he was never rambunctious around her.

And the most interesting thing happened. We had a large, oversized leather rocking chair. I'd shopped for it for months. It leaned slightly back and had overstuffed armrests that hugged Jan's stiff little body. She could sit alone in it.

Because of her cerebral palsy, Jan's limbs were stiff, and her skinny legs stuck straight out in front of her, hanging a bit off the rocker. Jake learned to back up under her feet and sit facing away from her. It was the cutest sight—Jake was Jan's perfect little footrest, and she was his back scratcher. Every time she coughed, which was often, the chair rocked as her body lunged forward. Jake thought she was deliberately rubbing him. That became one of his favorite places.

He was Ben's dog, but I'd never once expected that Jan would enjoy him so much. When we were in the backyard, she loved to hear his paws click-clack past her on the wooden deck, and she'd giggle. He'd run by her often or, at times, sit beside her panting, another sound that she loved. The tag on his dog collar also made a tinkling sound, and she delighted in hearing that too.

Jake loved it when we were all in the backyard. Unfortunately, high temperatures caused Jan to seizure, and sadly, as soon as the weather heated up, we spent most of the summer indoors.

> Jake loved it when we were all in the backyard.

We visited a grandparent in Florida who had a pool and were surprised to find that Jan dearly loved their pool, and, of course, Ben did too. We prayed about installing one, and when some old stock increased to the total cost of the pool, we felt we had our answer. In the coming days, as the pool was built Jake loved all the activity and digging going on in our yard. He'd watch from our sun porch and bark and, at the end of the day, scout out every single thing that had been done in the yard.

However, when the pool was finished and the water in, Jake really did not like the pool at all. He avoided it at all costs. I think he thought it was a big bathtub, and he hated baths. In fact, he made continual trips around the pool when we were in it, but always carefully on the outside rim of the sidewalk. He was taking no chances on falling in.

Our once long, hot summers of being indoors turned into many special family days. Jake delighted in all the activity around the pool, still, of course, avoiding being close to the water.

Eventually, we added a hot tub to our deck. It was covered by a heavy lid that was locked down when not in use. We built wide wooden steps up to the top. It appeared that Jake thought we built those wide steps just for him. It made it easy for him to scoot up onto the covered hot tub.

Jake learned that the covering on the tub was always on unless our family was in it, and that covering soon became his favorite perch to survey his kingdom, and us, as we swam. He'd run back and forth on his above-the-world-perch and then leap down the steps, run around the pool a few times, and then trot right back on top of the hot tub.

> The funniest of things occurred with Jake.

One year, in the early fall, the weather was still warm enough to invite Jan's class of ten for a swim party. All the kids were wheelchair-bound, and this was a big treat for them. Jake was so excited to have all the kids and laughter going on in our yard. He was meeting and greeting and sniffing everyone. In the midst of all the chaos, the funniest of things occurred with Jake.

I had removed the cover on the hot tub as the class arrived, and one teacher climbed in, holding a little girl. It never occurred to me that Jake would not know the cover was off. He was so enthusiastic over everything going on in his yard that after a bit, he decided to view it all from his favorite perch.

As I stood holding Jan, I caught a glimpse of a flash of movement. I realized it was Jake soaring up the steps to the hot tub top. He realized the lid was off just as he became airborne. All four of his legs spread out, and his hair stood on end as he attempted to put on the brakes. It was too late. He splatted into the middle of the hot water, landing right next to an extremely surprised teacher.

As Jake hit the water, the shocked teacher screamed, "Oh my goodness, your dog must really love the water."

I couldn't help but laugh because it was the complete opposite of what she thought. I dumped Jan into her wheelchair as fast as I could so I could rescue Jake. It turned out he didn't need my help. He scrambled over the edge of the hot tub, almost fell into the pool as he jumped out, and then ran for the bushes to hide. I felt so bad for him. He looked like a drowned rat. When he finally came out of the bushes, he let me love on him a bit, but I never again saw our poor doggie get on that hot tub lid.

THE TIME FLEW BY, AND soon Ben was off to college. And yes, it was me who took care of Jake, but that extra responsibility came with delight. Jake stood guard beside Jan on days that I worked in the flower beds as if she was his charge and he was guarding her. He excitedly greeted Ben when he came home from college, and he still made laps around the pool when we were in it—always on the outer edge.

When Jake was about twelve years old, we moved from the only home he'd ever known to a place that was near Ben and his budding family. Jake was not very excited about our new place because his ten-year routine was totally interrupted, and there was no pool to run around. On top of that, as he checked out every crevice and corner, he spotted himself in a mirrored, still-empty curio cabinet. I think that was almost the last straw for him. He thought not only had we moved, but he'd discovered another dog there. He barked ferociously and would not calm down. I had to quickly unpack the stuff to put in the cabinet so he could no longer see *that other dog*.

Jake lived to be fourteen years old, and it was a very sad day in our household when his health failed. We all grieved his absence.

Today, nearly twenty-four years later, I have three pictures of Jake that I love. One is of fifteen-year-old Ben holding his yet unnamed puppy. The next is of Jake sitting under Jan's feet, and the other is of Jake as a grayed little dog standing guard beside our first-born grandchild, Ben's son. They each have on golf hats that Grandpa purchased. Their names are embroidered on them—Jake and Jack.

What loyalty and love we would have missed if we'd never taken a chance on our little runt of the litter. He certainly blessed and enriched our lives. And to think, I balked for years about having that sweet addition to our family.

PAM WHITLEY TAYLOR is a wife, mother, and grandmother. She was a speaker for Christian Women's Club for many years. Both her testimony and writings share the tools she found to fight for hope, contentment, and joy in the midst of heartache and grief. Look for her book *God's Grace Keeps Pace* on Amazon. You can find her stories in several compilations, including Guideposts books. She now lives in Oklahoma with her sweet husband, John, where she enjoys photography and travel.

Paws with Promise

GAIL SCOATES

S HE CAUGHT ME AFTER THE church service ended. Marcia had something on her mind, judging by the brisk way she walked toward me.[3]

"Good morning, Gail. Where's Dave today?"

"He's off on a golf outing for a few days, but he'll be home on Thursday." As I went on to describe where he went, I could see she was anxious to tell me something.

"I have some news about a dog. I know you said you'd let me know when you were ready, but this can't wait. I have a special dog for you and Dave. She's a little over a year old and needs a home as soon as possible."

"But it's only been two weeks, Marcia. My heart isn't healed yet." Our twelve-year-old Golden Retriever, Max, had been receiving treatment for his bone cancer for the past two months. He was my first certified therapy dog, and together, we had completed over eight years of therapy dog work. But during our last visit for his cancer treatment, he eagerly greeted his helpers, and amid his

---

3.   This chapter first appeared in Gail's book. Gail Scoates, *Paws, Purpose, and Possibilities: How Therapy Dogs and Faith Healed my Heart* (Grato Publishing Company, 2022).

excitement, he jumped and fractured his leg. So, instead of getting treatment that day, we had to put him to sleep.

"I need to think about this some more. You and I both know how much I love my therapy dog work. And I will return to our church ministry. I've even been dreaming about all the things I can do when we get another dog. But it's going to take a few more weeks." I felt like I'd be cheating on Max, as if getting another dog so soon would somehow diminish my love for him.

"Please go and see her. If you're not sure, you can tell the couple that you'll think about it for a few days." Marcia was persistent. We talked for a while, and I told her I would mention it to my husband.

Marcia and I had met through our pet ministry at church, called P.A.W.S.—for Pets Are Working Saints. We'd hit it off right away—two ladies who loved our dogs and loved serving others. We both had Golden Retrievers, and that further glued our connection. She also worked for a Golden Retriever rescue and had access to dogs in need of a home. It was her mission to find a home for every dog that needed one.

> It was her mission to find a home for every dog that needed one.

When Dave called that evening, I told him about my conversation with Marcia. "I won't do anything rash. I know we said we'd wait before getting another dog."

"We don't need to hurry. Find out what you can and see if she'll be a good fit for your therapy dog work. If it's right, we'll pick her up when I get home." Dave is always calm and level-headed; he's the one who takes the high road while I go with my heart, sometimes a dangerous thing to do.

That night, all I could do was think about the dog. By the morning, I had convinced myself that it wouldn't hurt to go and look. I didn't have to bring the dog home. *The dog,* maybe if I didn't say her name, I could stay detached and uninterested.

About mid-morning, I drove to the address Marcia had given me. I parked in the driveway and sat there, not sure if I should go in. But I felt a push, and out I went. I knocked on the front door, and when it opened, I introduced myself.

"I came to meet Sadie. Marcia did tell you I was coming." It was as much a question as a statement. I found myself feeling surreal, as if someone else was doing this, not me.

The man nodded his head and said, "She did. Go ahead and meet me at the side door. I'll bring her out there."

> The side door opened suddenly with a crash, followed by a streak of gold.

The side door opened suddenly with a crash, followed by a streak of gold. "Easy, Sadie," the man shouted in the background. I took a few steps back to protect myself from this lunging, open-mouthed dog.

"She gets excited when she sees new people." What an under-statement. When the man finally got control of the dog, he tied her to a tree.

"She likes to run. We don't have a fence and don't have time to walk her. This was supposed to be our daughter's dog, but that didn't work out. We keep her in her kennel inside because she jumps on the furniture and is all over the kitchen counters. We'd like to find a home where she can run off her crazy energy." He went on to explain that Sadie had run away several times and, on one occasion, had been gone for days.

I scrutinized this young, very active dog, with her mouth gaping open and her tongue lolling out the side of her mouth as she hopped around. Her demeanor was not quite what I had dreamed of for my next therapy dog, as in calm, gentle, and obedient. I reminded myself that my husband and I were no spring chickens. He was already retired, and I wasn't long to follow. There were all sorts of reasons why this dog was simply not for us.

"Let me think about it, and I'll call you at the end of the week. I need to speak with my husband, but he's out of town for a few days." As we were talking, I tried to pet Sadie to get any clue if she enjoyed being touched and patted.

The man shook his head. "Well, that won't work. I thought you were going to take her. I promised my wife that Sadie would be gone today."

"Can't you keep her just a few more days? My husband needs to meet her before we make this commitment." I felt a gnawing sense of uncertainty and anxiety as I tried to envision what might happen next.

He shook his head no. "There's a guy in the country with lots of land where Sadie can run free. He said he'd take her if no one else wanted her. So, if you don't want her, I'll call him."

It's not that I didn't want her; it's just that I was having trouble envisioning this dog as a calm and obedient therapy dog.

At that moment, a neighbor walked over with his dog. It was evident that Sadie knew these neighbors, and I was taken aback at how engaged she was with this man and his dog. I began to wonder if there might be some redemption in Sadie after all.

> Right then, a quick prayer came into my heart.
> *Dear Jesus, forgive me for what I am about to do.*

Right then, a quick prayer came into my heart. *Dear Jesus, forgive me for what I am about to do.*

"I'll take her." I couldn't stomach the idea of this lovely dog running free in the countryside and maybe getting run over by a car or running in the woods and becoming lost.

With that, Sadie and her belongings were loaded into my car.

Oh my, what have I done? "Sadie, sit still. Sadie, settle down. Sadie, don't act so crazy!" While I shouted toward the back seat, she ran from side to side, jumping and attempting to come up front with me. It had never occurred to me to strap her in. My mistake. What a long ride home.

Once in the house, it was no different. She ran from room to room and jumped on everything. "Did I make a mistake bringing you home? What am I to do with you, crazy dog?" I felt a bit demented as I talked to the dog while she ran around the house.

In the process of watching Sadie running amuck, I began to regret my decision. I recalled how gentle and mellow Max had been and how easy it was to walk him on a leash even though he weighed eighty-five pounds. I wondered if it was even going to be possible for me to handle these sixty pounds of high-spirited golden energy.

> *Maybe I could just not tell him.* You know, evade the issue.

Panic engulfed me as I thought about the upcoming call with my husband. I said a quick prayer to give me the right words to say. I wouldn't lie. But a thought came to me: *Maybe I could just not tell him.* You know, evade the issue.

Dave called that evening and asked about Sadie. Focused on answering with the facts, I told him all I had learned upon meeting her. It's just the fact of her being home with me that never entered the conversation.

I attempted to side-step the truth the next night when he called, but it was evident that a confession was in order. "Okay, Dear, here's the real story. Sadie has been here with me since Monday. You never asked if she was here; you just asked questions about her." He laughed and told his golf buddies that Sadie was at the house. Their guffaws and teasing came through to my end of the phone as they carried on in the background.

He got a hoot out of my story. "I knew as soon as you saw her, you'd want to bring her home." Later, when he found out the neighbors had voted for Sadie to stay, he knew the decision had been made.

Sadie brought lots of activity and challenges to our home and kept us on our toes. We channeled her high energy with daily three-mile walks, dog classes, and playtime that never seemed to end. She continually entertained us with her never-ending energy.

"You are going to be a therapy dog, Sadie," I had told her the day I brought her home, wondering how that might ever be possible. But only a year and a half later, she became part of our church's P.A.W.S. ministry and earned her therapy dog certification. Today, nearing fifteen, she is celebrating close to twelve years of therapy dog work. We visit hospitals, schools, libraries, hospices, and residential homes for children. She has also helped me mentor almost fifty therapy dog teams in my role as a therapy dog evaluator.

I am grateful God opened my heart (and maybe gave me a push?) that day to bring her home with me. From runner to role model, from Crazy Sadie to Lady Sadie, she has brought great joy to our lives and the lives of others. Impossible? Only God can take the impossible and make it possible beyond our wildest imagination.

GAIL SCOATES is an award-winning author of *Paws, Purpose, and Possibilities: How Therapy Dogs and Faith Healed My Heart.* With a heart for God and for dogs, her books show us how God's creation can teach about God's love. A retired registered nurse, she also trains and evaluates teams for therapy dog work, writes, and travels. Gail is a member of the Advanced Writers and Speakers Association, Word Weavers, and the Christian Independent Publishing Association. www.pawspurpose.net

Ode to I-Pod

HALLY J. WELLS

We peered into the playpen
on the Aldi parking lot,
where several puppies skipped around,
but only one we sought.
All but one were smooth and slick;
they didn't have much hair.
But the woolly one *we* wanted
had lots of fur to spare!

We paid the eighty dollars
to bring our new pooch home,
but when we got him there,
we couldn't let him roam.
Poor guy had fleas tucked in his coat,
so to the vet we went.
We didn't want no critters
for the eighty we had spent.

Roz named the sweet thing I-Pod,
like her favorite device.
Perhaps, we should have taken time
to get good name advice.

I-Pod's not one type of guy;
he's two fine boys in one.
A Chihuahua and a Doxie
in one furry ball of fun!

When he was young, he'd sing with Roz—
all the way to school.
His head held out the window,
he was Super Doggie cool.
He annoyed his canine sister,
a dear, sweet Lab was she.
She tolerated I-Pod—
noisy pest that he could be.

Like his momma, I-Pod's feisty,
with a bit of attitude.
Like his momma, I-Pod lacks in legs
and also latitude.
Now, I-Pod is a fearsome friend;
his size can't hold him back.
If I-Pod thinks you mean us ill,
he ain't cutting you no slack!

When big boys used to stroll nearby,
"Pod" showed them he was boss.
We worried if he got chewed up,
we'd never heal from loss.
He'd yap and yap, and show his teeth,
so they would get the drift.
Our sassy, short protector
was a mess when he was miffed.

Like the music-making I-Pod,
our pup has gotten old.
His ears and eyes don't work too well;
he's not a fan of cold.
He's moved with us and made new buds
but likes his time alone.
He simply wants a cuddle spot,
a treat, and plastic bone.

At eighty-four in people years,
he's been with us twelve now.
We'd not trade him for a cat or horse
or Scottish Highland cow.
Since we spied him on that Aldi lot,
this funny, faithful friend,
I-Pod is the best Chiweenie
there has ever been!

HALLY J. WELLS is a retired school counselor, recent empty-nester, mental health advocate, and freelance writer. Hally writes on faith, parenting, and mental illness. Her three grown kids, along with many students, have awed and exhausted her in beautiful ways. Hally helps overwhelmed parents find practical answers, impactful resources, faith-family support, and divine wisdom—digging deep enough to find the good stuff, reaching high enough to find the best! Visit Hally at www.hallyjwells.com.

Chasing Bernie

LISA L. CROWE

W ITH BERNIE, IT WAS LOVE at first sight. I mean, how could you not be infatuated with that tiny ball of black fur? He weighed less than five pounds and you could hold him curled in your cupped hands. But he preferred to lay in your arms, nuzzled comfortably against your body.[4]

My friend Elaine had adopted the tiny long-haired Dachshund, and he was immediately the darling of our neighborhood. Born at the onset of the first lockdowns of 2020, he provided welcome comic relief. She named him Bernhart as a tribute to his German heritage and nicknamed him Bernie.

He might have been a handful, curled asleep in your lap. But he was more than a handful when he was awake. He was playful and smart and loved to play chase. He was also social to the point that he completely failed crate training. Elaine followed all the rules, placing the crate near her own bed and covering it with a blanket. And after five hours of his pitiful wailing, she finally gave up. He couldn't stand the isolation. And she needed sleep.

---

4. A similar version of this chapter first appeared online. Lisa L. Crowe, "Wanderlust," *Inspire a Fire* (blog), May 7, 2023, https://inspireafire.com/wanderlust/.

And he was fearless, playing for hours with a friend's Pit Bull mix who outweighed him by at least forty pounds. The first time I watched them together, I was biting my nails, sure that Lola, the Pit, would surely crush her tiny opponent. But she knew her limits, whether he knew his or not, and they enjoyed each other's company.

All the cuteness in the world didn't mitigate Bernie's persistent destructiveness. And after a while, Elaine grew tired of the trail of chewed-up hearing aids and computer cords and the trail of trash that he inevitably dragged through the house. She saw no end in sight and asked me if I wanted him.

> All the cuteness in the world didn't mitigate Bernie's persistent destructiveness.

Of course, I did. Soon, he was settling into his new home. My pack expanded to two. My senior hound, Daisy Mae, was content to ignore Bernie most of the time and put him in his place when necessary. She's not one to put up with nonsense. One sharp bark will usually send him scurrying for cover.

Bernie has always been an explorer. I guess it's his innate intelligence—and his perceptive nose. He has always been eager to strike out on his own, often trailed by a lead and a hapless pursuer who failed to hang on tight enough.

Last summer, my brother and I faced the daunting task of preparing our childhood home for sale. So, one Saturday, I loaded Bernie into the car and met Myron there to sort through a life-time's worth of stuff. At home, Bernie is contained by an in-ground fence, so he has the run of the yard. There, I had to tether him outside while I worked inside a shed.

I have learned not to ever ask, "What could go wrong?" when Bernie is involved. I assure you; he has an answer. And soon, the air was punctuated by emphatic yips. These were not barks of complaint for being left alone. Something was wrong.

I ran to check and found him wedged up against the foundation of the shed with his tether wrapped around multiple obstacles. I surveyed the mess and was formulating a plan to free him when he devised his own solution. He wriggled out of his harness and darted under the shed.

Myron heard my startled scream and raced to help, only to have Bernie slither free of his grasp and race to the wooded area behind Dad's property.

My heart sank as I realized Bernie's and my predicament. He had been to visit Dad with me a couple of times, but he had never been in those woods. Any woods, really.

There were a few houses around, but much of the area was overgrown with thick underbrush. The previous summer, there had been at least two different families of bear cubs. And years ago, my Basset Hound had nearly died from a rattlesnake bite while rabbit hunting.

> I took off after him, but I was no match for his speed and grace.

I took off after him, but I was no match for his speed and grace. His short legs and lithe body were ideal for navigating the rugged terrain, and he is a born hunter. I am a middle-aged, retired desk jockey. I was outmatched.

I could tell he was in hot pursuit of some small animal because I caught an occasional glimpse of him with nose to the ground, oblivious to all else around him. He might not be an apex predator, but he knows how to act like one.

Myron knows the lay of the land better than I do and jumped in his truck to try to intercept him further up the road while I tried to keep the little fugitive in sight without much success. I stopped long enough to catch my breath and update his AirTag status as lost, not that it did that much good. I now realized that I had misplaced confidence in the functionality of the AirTag. It could tell me where he had been, not his current location.

> For over an hour, we searched for him, and I was frantic.

For over an hour, we searched for him, and I was frantic. I could imagine dozens of fates—none of them good. I was beginning to imagine going home without him.

We had an appointment with someone at the house, so reluctantly, I turned back. I was trying to figure out how to post Bernie on the local missing dog page as I stood talking to one of Dad's friends when I heard Myron whisper, "There he is."

Startled, I looked up to see Bernie, less than twenty-five yards from where he had slipped from my grasp, digging frantically in soft soil. Dirt flew all around him, and he was oblivious to all except whatever creature lay burrowed beneath the surface.

He was a predictable criminal and had returned to the scene of the crime. Myron was closer, and I wordlessly handed him a treat. He crept closer until he caught Bernie's attention. Bernie warily sniffed the air and caught a whiff of the tasty morsel in Myron's hand.

He wanted it. But he also wanted his freedom. How could he have both? His intelligent eyes belied his dilemma. Finally, he got just close enough that Myron could tackle him, hugging Bernie's slim body close to his own. Bernie yelped in disappointment. But the chase was over, and he put up no protest while I put his harness back on and fastened it just a bit tighter. It's a game with Bernie.

He was filthy, matted with dirt and leaves, his beautiful black coat tangled with brambles, pine resin, and other debris. I didn't care. I hugged him close and kissed his dirty nose.

Later that evening, I bathed the little prodigal, painstakingly freeing his soft black coat of all the brambles and twigs. I swaddled him like a baby in a fluffy towel and sat cuddled with him for quite a while.

He dozed, and I imagined his dreams. Perhaps he saw himself triumphant over a monstrous bear, like a furry David and Goliath. But his contented sighs let me know he was happy right where he was.

I breathed a prayer of thanks to Father God. I know he protected Bernie on his expedition. And I thanked God, too, for all the times I had followed my desires into the wild, unaware of the dangers that lie out of sight. Yet God pursued me just like I pursued Bernie.

He's good like that.

LISA CROWE lives in the North Carolina mountains with her two dogs, Daisy and Bernie. Retired from state government, she directs the prayer team at her church, serves on the mission board, and leads women's Bible studies. She loves exploring her native mountains with her dogs and enjoys domestic and international travel. She is an avid reader, shares her insight on Facebook, and is a monthly contributor to *Inspire a Fire*, a blog maintained by Christian Devotions.

Hope in a Toad Hunter

DARCI WERNER

G ROWLING WAS NOT THE USUAL method of control for my Chihuahua and Miniature Dachshund blend—a tiny dog called a Chiweenie—who acted as if she viewed herself as a mighty Doberman. But here she was, her usual high-pitched bark replaced by a rumbling growl from deep within. She stood at attention on the lowest step of the short porch leading to the back door.

My mind drifted back to a year earlier, when we had lost our beloved German Shepherd mix that grew up with our son. We provided him a home when our son was in third grade. The pup had held out in failing health long enough to make it until our son could return from his sophomore year from his college campus to say their goodbyes. We had shared our life with him longer than any other animal we had owned, and it left a giant hole in my heart.

Life was full of adjustments. My husband and I were now empty nesters from the human standpoint as well as canines. I knew that jumping into having another pet would not be wise and continued life as normal for whatever context was "normal." In this timeframe, I lost a dear friend, my mother-in-law was passing, and our jobs were in peril from restructuring after COVID quarantines. My heart and spirit kept falling deeper into a dark pit with no glimpse of light in any direction.

In my heart, I had wanted a dog. For some reason, my soul and mind had a conversation and decided that having a canine back in the house was going to help ease my discomfort and spark a glimmer of hope back into our home.

THE GROWLING STOPPED FOR A brief moment, only to continue once again with a bit more attitude. I stopped my morning reading routine and went to investigate the situation. Our home is surrounded by farm fields with growth taller than Isla Mae. She stood tied to a cable that allowed her free access to roam at a distance from the door but not get lost. Or possibly encounter wildlife that would love her delicate frame for an appetizer.

"There is nothing there. I see nothing, Your Highness."

She stood at attention, pointing toward the outdoor chairs and small round table. I went back inside to finish my reading.

MY HUSBAND HAD NOT AGREED that we needed to bring a dog back into our lives. It took several weeks before I could convince him that it would benefit both of us. We settled on some ground rules. It would be an outside dog. No more dogs inside the house. We had to be careful of the breed due to having free-range poultry. Nor did we want to deal with training a young dog. I'd spent hours once a week looking at the surrounding dog shelters in our rural area. We filled out adoption forms whenever we spotted a possible match. One shelter denied our application because we live on a small acreage, and they wanted a completely fenced-in yard. All five acres of it. Another approved our entry on two elderly Rottweiler brothers that needed to stay together. We made preparations with beds and bowls and planned to drive an hour to pick them up. A call came as we headed out the door. Apologizing they said, "Someone locally has come in," and, since we did not reside in that county, "they will go to that family instead."

> My heart melted for this gentle giant as my husband fell head-over-heals in love with the pup.

The final shelter had an older male farm breed that was ready for adoption. He was found wandering local streets with a four-month-old black mixed pup. On the visit, the two were inseparable. A large Great Pyrenees and this little black energy ball resembling a mix of Labrador, Pit, and "who knows what." My heart melted for this gentle giant as my husband fell head-over-heals in love with the pup. The Pyrenees had a waiting list, and I was in third place.

The pup was not what we decided on. This playful pup did not check all the boxes we had settled on. With that, we went to the car to leave. Both of us stood at the car, unable to open the doors. We just could not leave her. We made a trek to the local coffee shop to discuss and ended up heading to the feed store for a dog bed and supplies.

THE COMMOTION AND GROWLING OUT back brought me back from reminiscing.

"Enough!" I grunted as I pushed myself away from the table. "Isla Mae! There is nothing out there." I made another trip out to console the beast.

And then, there it was! The monster that made her stand at attention at the bottom step, waiting to attack if it came close to her domain. She was my protector. My hero. It was hard for me to see with my human eyes, but her hawk-like vision saw the dangerous enemy that blended in the texture of the concrete sidewalk.

"Oh my! Stand back, Isla Mae," I said with a giggle. She was serious in protecting her home from this invading species. It was roughly two inches around on all sides, the gray and tan tones with its normal array of bumps. She growled even louder as it hopped across the sidewalk and leaped into a crack between the walk and house siding.

"Whew. That was close, Isla Mae. Thank you for protecting me from the big bad toad."

> Laughter came up quickly as the next attack phase took place.

Laughter came up quickly as the next attack phase took place. In trying to get my toad hunter to calm down, out from under the chairs came an even larger creature. The pup was ready, still in her defensive mode and on high alert. This one was about four inches long and scurried its fuzzy brown body toward us, stopping just a few feet from my fierce bodyguard. Its brown and white signature stripes adding a touch of style to the bold, chubby creature.

That signature growl gurgled up into her throat as a small dog and chipmunk face-off began. The rodent quickly turned and scurried back under the furniture and out into a grassy area. With some coaxing, my boundary patrol officer was put back into the house so I could finish my morning reading.

The entire time, she stood on guard at the patio door just in case they decided to reappear. The chubby chippie did decide to step back out into view and stirred a barking session for warnings. A quick retreat sent it up the nearest tree and out of sight. My fearless toad and chippie hunter was on duty.

IT HAD BEEN MY HEART that needed the hope, yet it was my husband's heart that was filled. He and his new little girl bonded instantly. She was "Daddy's little princess," and I was just the person that brought out the food. Our decision to house outside was now trumped with a cozy nook in the back hallway under the stairs.

Our jobs required varied time frames and were seldom the same. She was never left alone for very long. When she was, there were issues with anxiety. The days where she would be left longer than normal were the worst for her and for us. She needed a buddy. So, I went back to searching and found my favorite breed—Dachshund—at the same shelter. This one is all black with brown feet, chest, and snout. She resembles a dwarf Miniature Pinscher but has the longer body and deep chest of the Dachshund.

She is our Queen Chiween. Just as before, I could not leave. I knew in my heart that this little dog was to come home with me. She was my tiny spark that fanned into a flame and gave me hope for every morning.

> I knew in my heart that this little dog was to come home with me.

Our two canine girls were now buds. There was a size difference, but they managed. They always made sure they knew where each other was at and would be nervous if not close by. The one bed turned into two nestled in the cove with their own blankets and toys. Weeks went by as they settled into their new surroundings and became comfortable with us. As time passed, the "who knows what" DNA began to morph in our growing pup. Her head and body grew at normal proportions to her breed style, but the legs just kept stretching out longer and longer. Her hair color turning a silver undertone.

She was Great Dane. And the size variance was now comical between the two dogs.

MY READING ALSO INVOLVES JOURNALING. On this day, I thanked God for allowing me the chance to watch the interactions between his tiny creatures that seemed so small to me yet so big to my dog's tiny heart. To feel the warmth in laughter as the small dog shows the most ferocious behavior and the large breed just goes with the flow, adding in her two cents only when needed. They both have filled my heart again with a purpose, opened up the darkness, and allowed light to enter back in. Plus protected from invading toads or chippies!

DARCI WERNER lives in Northeast Iowa on a small hobby farm with her husband, dogs, ducks, and chickens. Faith and farm life fuels her passion for artwork and creative writing. She has published in Iowa-based magazines such as *LyricIowa*, Dubuque Writers Guild, and Magpie. Also including Mary Jane's Farm, Chicken Soup for the Soul, and Guideposts. She is currently a proud police wife (Retired) and writes for law enforcement publication *Blue Magazine*.

Fred, The Wonder Dog

JOHN TAYLOR

F I WERE A SONGWRITER, I would write a ballad about my dog Fred. In fact, I have several songs saved in my phone's music collection that artists have written about their beloved dogs. I enjoy listening to them because they remind me of Fred.

When we acquired Fred, it was the family who wanted him, not me. I didn't want to add more responsibility to our already busy schedule. After Fred had been in the house for a short time, he made me his human, and he quickly became my responsibility. He wouldn't obey anyone but me either.

In fact, others would give him a command, and he'd look at me as if to say, "Do I have to mind them?"

We lived in California at the time, and as with most backyards in the San Fernando Valley, there was a huge orange tree. When the oranges ripened and began to fall, Fred loved to eat them. I enjoyed watching him as he sat under that old orange tree. He'd choose which orange he wanted and then open it with surgical precision. He had a system. He'd use his front paws to stabilize the orange, and with his small front teeth, he'd carefully remove the top, and then he'd proudly devour the inside fruit.

Later, we moved to Oklahoma and built a house on an acre lot. It was a new subdivision, and we were one of the first houses built. The unfenced yard, surrounded by mostly empty lots, felt like we'd moved to the prairie. I loved it, and Fred loved it. He patrolled his new domain with delight.

> All twenty pounds of that little mutt were filled with tenacity and grit.

All twenty pounds of that little mutt were filled with tenacity and grit. He was a little dog with a big attitude. He had a shiny ebony coat, with ears that perched up yet gracefully flopped over halfway, and a fluffy tail that curled over his back as he pranced around, guarding his domain.

If a squirrel or rabbit dared to enter our yard, they'd better be prepared to run for their life because Fred could outrun them. To the critter's dismay, if Fred got a running start, he could run part way up the trunk of a tree as he chased them. That was a skill I'd taught him by wedging a tennis ball in a low tree branch or woodpecker hole, he'd get a running start and charge up the tree and grab it. He'd come back down and slowly destroy it, piece by piece—just as he did the oranges.

But nothing brought Fred into submission like my baby girl, Angie. She and Fred were two peas in a pod. When she was a baby with a bottle, I'd come through the house, and there was Fred, finishing off the milk in her bottle as he sat right beside her. As she grew older, I came home from work one day, and there was Fred in a doll stroller, dressed in baby clothes complete with a bonnet. He looked rather sheepish, but he loved Angie, so he tolerated it. However, Fred retaliated later and chewed up some of Angie's favorite toys. She chased him around the house, threatening him with time out, but she was never able to catch him. On another day, I looked around and saw Angie and Fred taking turns licking *their* ice cream cone. They were quite the pair.

Fred was not afraid of anything. Unlike most dogs, he loved the Fourth of July fireworks. He'd get excited and try to chase them. If we lit a spinner, we had to hold Fred because he was going to go after it, even if it burned his whiskers. He was not afraid of thunder and lightning either. He would bark and growl at it as if he was giving it fair warning that it aggravated him.

One of Fred's favorite things was a road trip. On a long one, he'd lie on the dash of our van, watching the sites as we traveled down the highway. In fact, anytime a vehicle door opened, Fred was ready to go. We learned we had to be very careful.

One day, a friend dropped her baby off so my wife could babysit. At some point when she was getting the baby out of her car, Fred silently sneaked into the vehicle. She didn't notice and drove all the way to work before she spotted Fred. He was sitting quietly in the back seat, enjoying his little adventure. She had to turn around and take him back home.

He also dearly loved camping and boating and literally traveled the country with us.

> The only two people he ever nipped were the mailman and the pizza delivery guy.

Fred loved people, but he was very protective of his best pal, Angie. The only two people he ever nipped were the mailman and the pizza delivery guy. They had the misfortune of getting between Angie and him and reaching toward her. That was unacceptable to Fred, and he let them know it.

We had other dogs through the years, but Fred ignored them totally. I always thought it was because he thought he was human.

He did, however, like the female dogs in the neighborhood. That often got him in big trouble. More than once in the night, he sneaked out our doggy door to go visit those neighborhood girls.

One such night, I awakened to a pitiful moaning sound. I hopped out of bed and found Fred hiding under the kitchen table. The poor thing was all chewed up. His fearless little personality had made him think he was as big as those hound dogs down the street. He found out differently.

I rushed him to the vet, and they stitched him back together. The doctor told us he would probably always walk with a limp. But he didn't count on the fact that Fred was a wonder dog. To everyone's surprise, Fred returned to normal and didn't let it slow him down one bit. He was soon back to his fearless little self. That late-night vet visit cost me a pretty penny, and the following week, I began installing a fence, but Fred was worth it.

Before I could complete the fence, Fred slipped out one more time on a girl-seeking mission, and the next morning, he was nowhere to be found. I knew something was wrong because he was always up and ready for his breakfast. After searching for him for hours, I called the dog pound.

"Is he a little black dog with a great big attitude?"

I had just started to give his description when the person on the phone asked, "Is he a little black dog with a great big attitude?" I knew I'd found him. They told me he was very aggravated at them for jailing him, and he'd refused their food. In fact, he would have nothing to do with them.

He was surely glad to see me when I rescued him, but he did seem embarrassed for a while about being a jailbird. I think he forgot about his incarceration when I took him to the vet for a little procedure that he didn't want. After that, he never chased the girls again.

Fred and I had several traditions. One was nightly. I always ate a bowl of cereal before I went to bed. Fred would patiently wait, sitting close beside my chair as I ate it. He knew that I'd leave a few bites back for him. When I'd eaten most of it, I'd put the bowl on the floor, and Fred enjoyed the remaining bites. He never ate dog food during the day but always held out for any people food he could get. Late at night, when he thought everyone was sleeping, we'd hear him crunching on his dog food. I guess he knew then there was no hope for people food.

Fred lived to be seventeen years old. I knew his days were numbered when I found him resting halfway through the doggie door. He was too weak to make it in one try. That broke my heart, and I knew it was time to let him go. On the day he died, I cried like a baby. Despite my initial reluctance to welcome Fred into our family, he proved to be an unwavering companion, during both my lowest valleys and highest mountaintops. I knew I'd never have another fur pup like him.

I buried Fred in our backyard—the same one where he'd chased the squirrels up the trees. Among the dog songs saved on my phone is one where a gal sings about burying her old dog beneath a tall oak tree. Inspired by that song, I planted a dogwood tree over his grave to forever mark where he was laid. He truly was the best dog I ever had.

JOHN TAYLOR worked for IBM as an IT guy for forty years, retiring in 2013. He is an avid photographer, enjoys woodworking, and loves traveling the country with his wife in their RV. His daughter, the one in this story, lives nearby with her hubby and their two pups. This is his first time to submit a story. He was egged on by his wife, Pam, because she felt Fred's story was too good not to share.

If I Were a Grandpawrent

MICHELLE RAYBURN

(*with a little help from Copper*)

MY NAME IS COPPER. I'M a Golden Retriever. I live on a country acreage with wonderful humans—a mom, a dad, and two preschoolers. The kids used to drop me lots of treats at meals, but they keep most of it on their plates now. My favorite food scraps are chicken and rice. But I'll eat just about anything—even vegetables or stinky rotten stuff.

We have chickens outside, but they are locked up in a coop, and we just stare at each other through the fence. Their beady eyes are kind of judgy, so I stay away. There are two cats, but sometimes we have twelve, and then we go back down to two again. Moms with minivans stop by with brown boxes and take kittens home. So far, no one has taken me in a box. Whew! And I can't tell what they are saying, but the humans have talked about the cats getting sprayed. Or throwing shade. Or was it spayed?

I have lots of space to find places to poop in private at my house, especially out by the row of pine trees past the apple orchard. I hate it when people watch me when I can't find my spot. Grandma gets annoyed with me and says I'm a persnickety pooper because of how many times I sniff and twirl, squat, sniff, twirl some more, and then try to find a new spot. It has to smell just right, and if it doesn't feel right or the grass pokes my bum, I start the squat sequence over again. And she wants me to go potty on a tie-out rope at her house. No dog can do his business with a silly rope in the way.

When I'm at Grandma's house, I don't like to be outside alone. I just stand on the steps and stare at the door until Grandma puts on her flip-flops and comes out with me. If it's raining, I take extra long to find my poop spot. Rain messes up the sequence and ruins the smells.

She says I cause her to get a lot of mosquito bites, but I don't notice any mosquitos. I think she makes that up because she wants to stay inside. Inside is nice and all, but the backyard is the best place. I can stand with my nose in the air for a long time, wiggling my nostrils and catching the scent of rabbits and squirrels. I think I smelled a porcupine, but Grandma stopped me from pursuing that. It might have been a bear, but after I stood up with my paws against the tree trunk, Grandma said it was time to go inside.

> Grandma is super nice to me, and I love her.
> She gives the best face massages.

Grandma is super nice to me, and I love her. She gives the best face massages. Grandpa looks disgusted when she scratches my back and not his. She doesn't complain about my breath or my stinky ears either. If Grandpa had stinky breath and ears, she would let him know right away.

One time, our cat—Grandpa calls her Walter because of some TV commercial—sneaked into Grandpa's truck and rode all the way to the forest with him. Dad and Grandpa were cutting firewood when they heard Walter meowing from inside the back of the truck. I haven't figured out how to sneak into Grandpa's truck yet. He stops over a lot because he lives just up the road. But I'm a big hairy beast, and he would notice if I hopped into his Chevy. He lets me ride up front sometimes to go to his house to visit Grandma. When I'm staying with him and Grandma, I ride home with Grandpa to check on the chickens and the cats.

My life is pretty happy, and I get the zoomies when anyone asks if I want to go for a ride. But if I were a grandpawrent, I'd do a few things differently.

> Grandma has some peculiar rules, none of which I understand or respect.

Grandma has some peculiar rules, none of which I understand or respect. There's a "no dogs on the couch" rule that I have learned to interpret as "no dogs on the couch if Grandma doesn't know about it." She piles on laundry baskets and boxes before she goes to bed, but if she misses a corner, I find a spot to curl up. If I were a grandpawrent, I wouldn't put anything on the couch. Anyone could sleep there, even in Grandma's special spot.

There is also a problem with the trash can. Grandma usually has it uncovered, but when I come over, she puts a lid on it. If I were a grandpawrent, I would leave it uncovered forever. The best late-night snacks are in there. It's no fun if I can't sniff around between the papers to look for scraps of chicken wings or mac and cheese.

If I were a grandpawrent, no dog would ever have to be on a leash in the backyard. It severely hinders exploration. Those rabbits taunt me from just outside of range. I'd really like to know where they hide! There's also this black-and-white furry guy with a long tail that looks interesting. I haven't been able to make friends. Grandma probably doesn't like it because he smells like he rolled in cannabis leaves. Grandma has weird rules about rolling in stuff.

Grandpawrents should have set times every day for throwing the ball. A few hours would do. These current short bursts of time are nonsense. That isn't play at all. I've discovered that older people are a bit boring. It wouldn't hurt if Grandma moved a little more. I could be the Chief Fitness Trainer if she just let me.

I know Grandma has a soft spot for me, but she doesn't share very well. She eats brownies or chocolate ice cream and never shares any with me. This stuff about chocolate being poisonous to dogs is probably like my pawrents telling the preschoolers the candy is spicy and, "You wouldn't like it." I propose a new "unlimited treats" rule to test it out.

> If I were a grandpawrent, I would let granddogs sleep *in* the bed.

When I stay over, Grandma makes me a sleeping spot in the living room with a folded blanket on the floor. It's one of my human dad's old bedquilts with motorcycles printed on it. It still smells like Dad. But if I were a grandpawrent, I would let granddogs sleep *in* the bed with the humans. I know I'm big and furry, but there should always be room. And I wouldn't get mad if a pup started licking his paws during the night.

After Grandma goes to sleep, I sneak into the hallway and stay outside her door. If she forgets to close the guest room door, I stay across the hall in a comfy secret spot. Shh! Don't tell.

Just last week, I visited Grandma when she was working on editing a book for people who love dogs and cats. I love dogs and cats. She asked if we should have more stories about cats, and I shook my ears. Definitely not. Cats have all the territory they already need.

You know, if I were a grandpawrent, I'd do a lot of what my grandma already does. I'd get excited when the humans and the pup come over. I'd give ear rubs and kiss the pooch's face—and kiss the kiddos too. Why not? "Share the love" is my motto. We would do doggie spa time and brush and brush my fur until I fell asleep in the cool grass under the pine tree. We would go for rides and roll down the windows and eat corn chips and cheese.

Grandma greets me as if I'm the most special dog in the world. Her scratches are spot-on, and visiting her house feels like a mini-vacation every time. If I were a grandpawrent, I'd be like her. Hey, Grandma? Can I have some cheese now? I was a good boy while you wrote this for me.

Copper

MICHELLE RAYBURN, the publisher and managing editor of this book, is married to her high school sweetheart, Phil, is mom to two thirty-something sons, and adores their wives. She has four grandchildren—and counting. Michelle hosts the *Midlife Repurposed* podcast and writes humor, Christian living books, and Bible studies. Dark chocolate, an iced coffee, and a good book in the hammock top her favorites list—especially if there's a visiting pup to watch bunnies and squirrels and share the backyard.

Thank You

AS THE MANAGING EDITOR OF this anthology, I am deeply grateful to each of the contributors who have shared their creativity and love for our four-legged friends. Your wonderful stories have brought this collection to life, celebrating the unique bond we share with pets and the lessons we learn from them.

Thank you for pouring your heart into every word and for making this project a true testament to the joy, comfort, and laughter that dogs and cats bring into our lives. This book is a treasure because of you.

To our readers, thank you for picking up this collection and for being kindred spirits who understand the special connection between humans and their pets. Whether you've laughed, cried, or found comfort within these pages, we're grateful to share in the universal love of animals with you. Your support of these stories helps keep alive the joy and companionship our furry friends give us every day.

With appreciation,

Michelle

If you have enjoyed this book, look for other collections at
FCLBooks.com

Made in the USA
Columbia, SC
08 February 2025

52943532R00129